AND YOU CALL YOURSELF A CHRISTIAN?

Answering the Common Misconceptions About Christianity

Everett Leadingham, Editor

Though this book is designed for group study, it is also intended for personal enjoyment and spiritual growth. A leader's guide is available from your local bookstore or your publisher.

Beacon Hill Press of Kansas City
Kansas City, Missouri

Copyright 2001
by Beacon Hill Press of Kansas City

ISBN: 083-411-9226

Printed in the
United States of America

Editor: Everett Leadingham
Assistant Editor: Charlie L. Yourdon
Executive Editor: Randy Cloud

Editorial Committee: Philip Baisley, Randy Cloud, Valerie Hall,
Everett Leadingham, Tom Mayse, Larry Morris, Darlene Teague,
Richard Willowby, Mark York, Charlie Yourdon

Cover design: Michael Walsh
Cover art: Keith Alexander

10   9   8   7   6   5   4   3   2

Contents

Introduction

Most of us have a list of actions and ideas that we consider to be "unchristian." If we see or hear someone do or say one of the things on our list, we might be tempted to say, "And you call yourself a Christian?"

Most of us have such lists. However, the interesting thing is that our lists are different. We might assume that all the lists are the same. After all, Christians believe the same things, right? Well, no, not exactly. That's one of the things this book is about—looking at the ideas we have about Christianity.

Of course, Christians are not the only ones who make observations about Christian behaviors and attitudes. Those outside the church also have opinions about people who go to church. They are not necessarily shy about saying what those opinions are. But when we look closely at what they say, we realize that often they are operating with a faulty set of ideas when they make judgments about Christianity.

The world's negative opinions do not always stay outside the church. Often in extremely subtle ways, the world's wrong ideas creep into the thinking of Christians. The criticisms may get stated inside the church in a way that sounds reasonable to Christians, but they are often the world's views dressed up in sheep's clothing.

In this book we examine 13 such faulty ideas or misconceptions that people—believers as well as unbelievers—may have about Christianity. We compare each one to the truth of Scripture and learn how Christians can refute the wrong ideas effectively.

It should be an interesting process, sorting out the true from the sounds-like-true statements. Some criticisms are easily seen as false; others require considerable thought and prayer. So grab your Bibles and let's learn how to respond if someone, somewhere, someday walks up to you and says, "And you call yourself a Christian?"

Common Misconception No. 1

Heard Outside the Church: "The Church never questions itself."
Heard Inside the Church: "Christians should not question their faith."

Background Scripture: Genesis 1:2; Job 13:15; Psalm 22:1; Isaiah 1:18; Matthew 7:7-8; Mark 9:23-24; 10:12; John 14:6, 17; 15:26; 16:13; 20:25, 28; Romans 1:17; 2 Corinthians 3:6; 5:13; 6:14-18; 13:5; 1 Timothy 4:6; 6:3; 2 Timothy 1:13; 4:3; Titus 1:9, 13; 2:8; Hebrews 11:6; 1 John 4:1; Revelation 22:17

CHAPTER 1

The Questioning Tradition of the Church

by C. S. Cowles

"Our new pastor is so neat," she enthused. "He doesn't preach all that theology jazz; he just preaches the Bible."

Little did that college sophomore realize that in setting theology over against the Bible, she was reflecting not a biblical but a secular worldview. She assumed that the Bible has to do with faith—which it does, and theology with reason (rational discourse about God)—which it does. Her questionable assumption was that these are incompatible. That is precisely why our sophisticated, scientific, technological age dismisses religion out of hand—namely, faith and reason have nothing to do with each other. It assumes that while science is built on the solid foundation of reason, faith operates in the netherworld of irrational superstitions and myths.

Indeed, faith and reason seem mutually exclusive in that the first principle of the scientific method, according to 17th-century thinker René Descartes, is, "Everything must be doubted until it is proven true." The first principle of biblical religion, on the other hand, is that "without faith it is impossible to please God, because anyone who comes to him *must believe* that he exists and that he rewards those who earnestly seek him" (Hebrews 11:6, emphasis added). Biblical revelation begins and ends with the assumption that God is. That

God exists can neither be verified nor contradicted by scientific proof.

Since faith lies beyond the reach of reason, it is therefore immune to probing questions, forthright challenge, and careful examination.

Or is it?

Faith and Reason

To set faith over against reason is artificial at best, and dangerous at worst. Scientists cannot prove anything apart from faith: that is, they must have faith that they can think, faith in their powers of observation and logical analysis, and faith that there is an intelligible coherence to that which they are examining. These presuppositions are themselves beyond the reach of testing and proof. No lab experiment has yet been devised that can prove that human beings are rational. Indeed, it might be asked: What's reasonable about building bombs that can destroy the world in one blast? What's rational about unrestrained scientific, industrial, and technological "progress" that consumes, pollutes, and poisons our fragile planet?

To assume, on the other hand, that since faith lies beyond reason, we should not exercise reason in questioning faith claims is not only foolhardy but may be dangerous as well. "Oh, Pastor," a 65-year-old parishioner exclaimed over the phone, "while visiting my son's church, I claimed healing by faith alone. I've thrown away all my medications." Knowing that she was a diabetic and dependent upon daily injections of insulin, my heart sank. Three weeks later, I held her funeral. It never occurred to her that she had thrown away the very means God had provided for the maintenance of her health. "An unexamined life is not worth living," said Socrates. Experience teaches us that an unexamined faith can be deadly.

There was another assumption that the college sophomore made, reflective of the anti-intellectual mind-set of many believers—namely, all one needs for the life of faith is to "believe the Bible." "Why are you going to seminary?" my revered preacher-father asked. "You've already been to Bible college. What more do you need?" He was worried that more education would destroy my faith. Yet even at that young age, I could see not only that the Bible was the Word of life, but also that the Scriptures could do a great deal of damage when misinterpreted and disconnected from sound thinking.

Sharon, one of the most sincere and earnest believers in our congregation, sat ramrod straight on the edge of her chair in my office. Through clenched teeth she forced out the words: "Pastor, God is testing my faith as He did Abraham. He is asking me to offer my four-year-old son as a sacrifice." For four unbroken hours I tried to dissuade her. My probing questions, moral and ethical objections, and citations of other scriptural passages seemed, in her mind, so puny next to the towering faith of Abraham—a faith that God would either provide a substitute sacrifice or resurrect his slain son. Only our proactive intervention and her total psychotic break later that afternoon stopped her from killing her son. My wife and I sat on either side of her—straitjacketed and babbling incoherently—in the back of a police car as it sped 75 miles through the night to the nearest mental hospital.

If active persecution of believers by an unbelieving world has slain its thousands, the misuse and abuse of Scripture has slain its tens of thousands. I have close relatives who have devoted their entire lives to missionary work. Yet when their oldest daughter got a divorce from a physically abusive husband and then remarried, they cut her out of their lives, citing Mark 10:12 and 2 Corinthians 6:14-18. Since then they have not visited, written, or called her, and have returned her letters unopened. Recently, she learned from her sister that their father had suffered a heart attack and had undergone multiple-bypass surgery. Immediately, she phoned home. Her mother hung up on her.

The apostle Paul knew all too well, from his own self-righteous preconversion experience, that "the letter kills" (2 Corinthians 3:6c). Paul went on to exclaim, however, that "the Spirit gives life" (v. 6d). What Spirit? The gracious Holy Spirit whom Jesus describes as "the Spirit of truth" (John 14:17;

15:26; 16:13). The truth that the Spirit personifies stretches from the dawn of creation when "the Spirit of God was hovering over the waters" (Genesis 1:2) to the end of time when "the Spirit and the bride say, 'Come!'" (Revelation 22:17), and encompasses everything in between.

The truth of God's Word is not to be found in isolated texts lifted out of context. Or cobbled together according to whim or prejudice. Rather, it is the vast truth of salvation history that comes to its fullness in Jesus, who himself is "the way, *the truth,* and the life" (John 14:6, KJV, emphasis added). John spoke of Jesus as being the *logos,* the Word, which in the Greek language means not only a vehicle of communication but also the spirit of reason, coherence, and intelligibility—that which makes sense. Jesus is the supreme incarnation of rationality. The truth that is in Jesus goes beyond reason but is never contrary to reason.

That is why Isaiah pleaded, "'Come now, let us *reason* together,' says the LORD" (1:18, emphasis added). And why the apostle Paul described believers again and again with phrases that result from a reasoned faith: "right mind" (2 Corinthians 5:13); "good teaching" and "sound instruction" (1 Timothy 4:6; 6:3); "sound teaching" and "sound doctrine" (2 Timothy 1:13; 4:3; Titus 1:9); "sound in the faith" (Titus 1:13); and "soundness of speech" (2:8).

John Wesley said, "It is a fundamental principle with us [as Christians] that to renounce reason is to renounce religion, that religion and reason go hand in hand, and that all irrational religion is false religion."[1] There is crazy faith and rational faith. Crazy faith says that I can jump out of an airplane without getting hurt, while rational faith says that if I have a parachute when jumping out of an airplane, the chances are excellent I will make a safe landing.

The faith to which the Bible leads us is a reasonable faith grounded firmly in the great saving works of God in history, which reach their apex in the death and resurrection of Jesus Christ. Everything in Scripture must be evaluated in the light of the teaching of the whole of Scripture as it finds its clearest expression in God's full self-disclosure in Jesus. That is the task of theology, and why we need to question, examine, and evaluate every religious claim in the light of that overarching truth.

Faith and Doubt

It would seem that doubt is the mortal enemy of faith. Philip Yancey, a best-selling Christian author, writes that when he was asked to sign *Christianity Today* magazine's statement of faith "without doubt or equivocation," he had to admit, "I can barely sign my own name without doubt or equivocation."[2]

Such it was with the disciple Thomas. He felt, in the light of the Crucifixion, that he had bet his life on Jesus and lost. So we can understand his skepticism when his fellow disciples told him that they had seen the Lord. "He said to them, 'Unless I see the nail marks in his hands and put my finger where the nails were, and put my hand into his side, *I will not believe it*'" (John 20:25, emphasis added).

That the risen Lord even appeared to him at all clearly indicates that He was not put off by Thomas's lack of faith. To the contrary, doubt may well have been his handmaiden to faith. When he saw the Lord, he did not need to put his finger in His nail prints nor thrust his hand into His side. Rather, with his heart bursting in love and devotion, he cried out, "My Lord and my God!" (v. 28).

Thomas went on, according to the lore of tradition, to become a missionary. He journeyed as far east as the subcontinent of India, where he died as a martyr for the faith, but not before he had established a flourishing church that has survived for 2,000 years, known today as the Martoma (Thomist) Church of South India.

As we read through the Bible, we see that doubt often coexists with faith. Abraham, a great hero of faith, so doubted God's promise of a son that he took things in his own hands and sired a son by Hagar, Sarah's Egyptian handmaiden. Doubting God's protecting power, twice he palmed off his wife as his sister, each time putting her in moral jeopardy.

Though "the patience of Job" has become an oft-repeated phrase, the Book of Job tells a different story. He was plagued by doubts over God's goodness and power at every point. His great faith was not the absence of doubt but triumph in the midst of doubt. "Though he slay me, yet will I hope in him" (13:15).

Other great religious figures have struggled in this area as well. Martin Luther, for whom the cornerstone of the gospel was "The righteous will live by *faith*" (Romans 1:17, emphasis added), constantly battled doubts about his faith. At the height of the great Evangelical Revival that was sweeping across England, John Wesley went through a period of such doubt that he questioned everything he was preaching and wasn't even sure he was saved. One is hard-pressed to find an autobiography of great people of faith in which they do not confess to passing through deep waters or what St. John of the Cross described as "the dark night of the soul."

It is only as faith passes through the fire of doubt, examination, and questioning that it is clarified and purified. Frederick Buechner writes that a relationship between an invisible God and visible humans will always involve an element of uncertainty. "Without somehow destroying me in the process, how could God reveal himself in a way that would leave no room for doubt? If there were no room for doubt, there would be no room for me."[3]

Faith Seeking Understanding

When Jesus came down from the Mount of Transfiguration, He found a man in the crowd desperate for the healing of his demon-possessed son. Jesus said to him, "Everything is possible for him who believes." The poor man responded, "I do believe; *help me overcome my unbelief!*" (Mark 9:23-24, emphasis added).

The poet Emily Dickinson rightly observes, "We both believe, and disbelieve a hundred times an hour, which keeps believing nimble."[4] Questions are the constant companion of faith in the life of the growing, thinking believer.

And that is all to the good, for the enemy of faith is not

doubt but naïveté. One of my friends from childhood days excitedly shared with me many years ago, after hearing a popular "health, wealth, and prosperity" preacher, that he had decided to adopt the seed-faith financial principle—which is, if you want to double your income, double your tithe. He did better than that; he began to triple-tithe, not on the net income from his small business but on the gross receipts. Six months later, the tax authorities moved in, padlocked his business, auctioned off his assets, and slapped him with back taxes, fines, and penalties that would take him 30 years to pay off. In bitter disappointment, he abandoned the church and the faith.

When we look around and see the smorgasbord of bizarre beliefs, strange cults, and get-rich-quick schemes in which people blindly place their faith, we begin to see that asking critical questions can be our best friend in protecting us from bogus claims and self-destructive traps. "*Examine* yourselves," counseled Paul, "to see whether you are in the faith; *test* yourselves" (2 Corinthians 13:5, emphases added). "Dear friends," John the beloved apostle wrote, "do not believe every spirit, but *test* the spirits to see whether they are from God, because many false prophets have gone out into the world" (1 John 4:1, emphasis added). Doubt is faith with its eyes wide open.

There is a book titled *The Encyclopedia of Ignorance*. While most encyclopedias compile information that is known, this book deals with areas of science and human consciousness not yet explained. What exactly is curved space-time? or time itself? How is the brain able to sort through over 100,000 pieces of stimuli received through the five senses each day and determine which to ignore, such as the sight of clouds floating overhead, and which to act upon, such as the sound of a ringing phone?

It seems that God has an "Encyclopedia of Theological Ignorance" full of fenced-off areas. What about the fate of those who have never heard the gospel? Why are some prayers answered, but many are not? If God is in total control, then why do so many things seem out of control? Why doesn't God intervene when a five-year-old girl is being raped, beaten, and killed? If God knows all futures exhaustively as if they were past history, then why pray or why evangelize?

Though God breaks His silence and finally speaks to Job at the end of his long and torturous spiritual journey, He does not answer the question that is central to the whole story: "Why do bad things happen to good people?" The Bible is endlessly fascinating in that it presents us with questions and answers. It reveals *and* conceals.

It is surely a mark of God's grace that while He has revealed everything necessary for our salvation and for growth in holiness, there are vast areas of truth where we hear only faint whispers, see dim reflections, and discover subtle hints into the meaning of dark mysteries. And that's what keeps stretching us.

We are called to the scary but intriguing life of what Anselm, a medieval church theologian, called "faith seeking understanding." John Donne has a thought-provoking line in one of his poems: "Churches are best for prayer that have least light."[5] The churches that resist the siren call to spell out what God himself has not disclosed, and that leave plenty of room for mystery, are more conducive to worship. It is only when the night is the darkest that we see the galaxies splayed out against the heavens most clearly.

Charles H. Spurgeon, who for 30 years preached to thousands every Sunday in a London church, tells of passing through a terrible time of doubt and depression. On the Sunday night before taking a four-month leave of absence from his pulpit, he preached on Jesus' cry from the Cross, "My God, my God, why hast thou forsaken me?" (Psalm 22:1, KJV). He said that he entered that text as completely as possible that night. Following the service, a man rushed up to him in a state of extreme distress. He told Spurgeon that he had been on his way to the Thames River with a revolver in his pocket, intending to end it all. As he walked by the church, he heard Spurgeon announce his text. He felt that anyone who could preach on that subject from personal experience would understand him. As they talked, Spurgeon led him to Christ.

Many years later, that same man approached him at a ministerial conference. His appearance had so changed that Spurgeon didn't recognize him. He said that he had been living in the sunshine of God's love ever since that night. Now he, too, was a pastor, leading a thriving congregation. Spurgeon concluded from that encounter that he would be willing to go into the valley of doubt and depression a thousand times if it helped one person find the way out of darkness into the light of Christ.

Conclusion

So, we return to the questions with which we began. Should we, as the Church, ask questions about faith? The answer is definitely yes. Do we have to live in constant, debilitating despair because of questions? No. Is Christianity rational? Yes and no. Our faith is informed by intelligent thought, but simply understanding concepts is not the basis for our faith. However, we know faith that seeks understanding will be rewarded. Jesus said, "Ask and it will be given to you; seek and you will find; knock and the door will be opened to you. For everyone who asks receives" (Matthew 7:7-8).

Notes:

1. "To Dr. Rutherford," 28 March 1768, *Letters,* in *The Works of John Wesley,* ed. Frank Baker and Richard P. Heitzenrater (Oxford: Clarendon Press, 1975), 5:364.

2. Philip Yancey, *Reaching for the Invisible God* (Grand Rapids: Zondervan Publishing House, 2000), 41.

3. Ibid., 42-43.

4. Ibid., 37.

5. Ibid., 46.

About the Author: Dr. Cowles is a religion professor at Point Loma Nazarene University in San Diego.

Common Misconception No. 2

Heard Outside the Church: "Christians
   don't make good scientists."
Heard Inside the Church: "Education
   can ruin your faith."

Background Scripture: Job 1:3, 13-19;
   2:9; 13:15; Psalm 34:8; Acts 17:11-12; 1
   Corinthians 3:18-19; 13:12; Philippians 2:12-16; 1 Thessalonians 5:21; 1
   Timothy 4:12-13, 15-16

CHAPTER 2

Intellectual or Christian: Is That the Choice?

by Cheryl Gochnauer

A stone wall.

That's what many nonbelievers figure they'll run into when they try to talk about real-life issues—like politics, women's rights, and scientific advances—with Christians.

"Bible-thumpers don't think for themselves. In fact, they're usually against any kind of progressive, intellectual argument. Can't imagine a Christian in a laboratory. He or she might run into something in the middle of an experiment that would mess with his or her mind. Give 'em that old-time religion; it's good enough for 'em."

Immediately, believers' backs go up.

"Not fair! We're not closed-minded; we're just prudent. We're supposed to be *in* the world without being *of* the world. People need to be careful about what they allow into their minds, hearts, and homes. It is better to stay away from anything that even whiffs of wickedness. After all, open yourself up to wrong teachings, and who knows where you'll end up?"

Good point. But how do we avoid that old cliché of "throwing the baby out with the bathwater" as we search for truth while shunning evil?

Hurdling the Herd Mentality

First, we need to know *why* we believe what we believe.

Living in a Christian nation, growing up in a Christian home, or surrounding ourselves with Christian friends doesn't make us Christians. The blessing of being born into a Christian family can easily be offset if someone bases his or her faith on heredity instead of experience. There's a reason why they call it "a *personal* relationship with Jesus Christ." This special bond between humans and their Maker is individual, sacred, and precious. To skip the intimacy is to miss the still, small Voice that is so important in helping us think through the very issues that challenge us.

There is also a danger in automatically chiming along with the most strident voices when discussing cultural issues. Any African-American whose ancestors were enslaved can testify that an act can be lawful and still be wrong. Truth is dictated by God, not the majority. "Do not deceive yourselves," we read in 1 Corinthians. "For the wisdom of this world is foolishness in God's sight" (3:18-19).

Instead, the Bible encourages us, with minds open to the Lord, to "continue to work out your salvation with fear and trembling, for it is God who works in you to will and to act according to his good purpose. Do everything without complaining or arguing, so that you may become blameless and pure, children of God without fault in a crooked and depraved generation, in which you shine like stars in the universe as you hold out the word of life" (Philippians 2:12-16).

The Word gives us clear insight into Christ's character. "Work out your salvation" indicates that we should carefully examine challenging ideas, basing our responses on what we know to be true of God.

When a puzzling theory arises, let's face it in a thoughtful manner, rather than with immediate resistance or acceptance. Acts 17 describes the apostle Paul's journey through Thessalonica, Berea, and Athens. Look how the Berean Christians are portrayed as they pondered the new theological ideas Paul preached in their synagogue: "Now the Bereans were of more noble character than the Thessalonians, for they received the message with great eagerness and examined the

Scriptures every day to see if what Paul said was true. Many of the Jews believed, as did also a number of prominent Greek women and many Greek men" (vv. 11-12).

There's the key. They "examined the Scriptures . . . to see if what Paul said was true." We should do the same today, no matter what troubling allegation or exciting revelation comes our way.

Faith the Facts

"Test everything. Hold on to the good."

Sounds like excellent advice, and it is—straight from God's Word in 1 Thessalonians 5:21. It is a way of life for dedicated scientists and inventors around the world, who spend their careers testing, tossing, and holding on to the good.

Thanks to their perseverance and God's grace, the world is full of amazing medical and technical advancements. Innovative vaccines, medical operation techniques, machinery, and microchips have revolutionized our lives.

Still, human knowledge is not perfect, no matter how confident some clinicians may appear. The scientific discovery process can be agonizingly slow, and with the passage of time, many former "facts" have been discredited. Despite classic examples of information once thought to be true, we know:

❏ The world isn't flat.

❏ The sun doesn't revolve around the earth.

❏ And the world's computers didn't scramble at 12:01 A.M. on New Year's Day, 2000.

A persistent prejudice claims that most highly educated professionals—scientists, doctors, professors—don't believe in God. Yet, faith and fact don't have to be mutually exclusive. As a matter of *fact*, experiments are actually perfect examples of faith in action.

Just think about it: A scientist makes an assumption, then sets out to prove it. The scientist possesses the faith that his or her assumption will prove itself over the long testing process. Years pass; elements of the study are tweaked and examined, then tweaked again. Once a breakthrough of knowledge occurs, then the completeness of understanding unfolds. But until that breakthrough, the scientist holds on in faith to his or her initial hypothesis.

Christian parents commonly fear sending their graduating high school seniors off to colleges and universities. "Don't let those educators ruin your faith," they admonish, eyeing a perceived sea of too-open-minded professors. However, along with unfairly prejudging their teachers, this attitude assumes our Christian young people aren't capable of thinking for themselves.

The best preparation for turning our kids loose in the world is to train them up in God's Word, filling them with practical, scriptural spirituality. Look at how Paul encouraged Timothy, who had blossomed under the religious tutoring of his faithful mother, Eunice, and grandmother, Lois: "Don't let anyone look down on you because you are young, but set an example for the believers in speech, in life, in love, in faith and in purity. Until I come, devote yourself to the public reading of Scripture, to preaching and to teaching. . . . Be diligent in these matters; give yourself wholly to them, so that everyone may see your progress. Watch your life and doctrine closely. Persevere in them, because if you do, you will save both yourself and your hearers" (1 Timothy 4:12-13, 15-16).

The ability to listen objectively to others' views lies in watching "life and doctrine closely" as we seek points where faith and fact intersect. But take care! Positions that appear to or do conflict can easily polarize people, spark hostility, and close the door for future dialogue.

When God Doesn't Pick Up the Phone

What do we do when we've faced our questions, done our research, and still don't find any clear-cut answers?

We each go through periods when reasons remain elusive. The Book of Job is a fascinating account of one man's struggle through a series of devastating events. God was pleased with Job's devotion and had blessed him with a large family, riches, and a reputation as "the greatest man among all the people of the East" (1:3).

At the height of Job's success, God allowed Satan to destroy everything Job held dear. His flocks and herds were stolen or zapped with lightning. His servants were killed. The house where his 10 children were celebrating collapsed, and they all died (see vv. 13-19).

Job's own health was threatened as Satan struck him with painful sores from head to foot. His support team broke down when three friends came to comfort him, but instead ended up accusing Job of sinning and bringing all this upon himself. Even his wife threw in the towel, saying, "Curse God and die!" (2:9).

From what he could see, Job hadn't done anything to anger God. Though he questioned why these tragedies were coming his way, he refused to blame God for them. Throughout the ordeal, Job trusted God with his life: "Though he slay me, yet will I hope in him" (13:15). In the end, the Lord restored Job's riches, giving him twice as much as he had before, and also blessed him with 7 sons and 3 daughters.

It can be tough to keep the faith when we're blinded by a situation. First Corinthians 13:12 encourages us to hold on, waiting for God's perfect timing: "Now we see but a poor reflection as in a mirror; then we shall see face to face."

While we're waiting for facts to emerge from faith, we shouldn't be afraid to ask "why"—respectfully, of course. God is not intimidated by our queries. Since He loves to give good things to His children, we can be confident that He will eventually reveal all we need to know. The key is to trust God with the timing of that revelation, whether in this life or the next.

Sighted Faith

Christians are often accused of depending upon blind faith. That is a fallacy; blind faith is not faith at all. Even the faith exhibited in the first moments of conversion is based upon an unarguable fact revealed to us by the Holy Spirit: that we have sinned, fallen short of God's requirements, and need Christ as our Savior.

How do we maintain faith? In addition to the comforting influence of the Holy Spirit, faith is nurtured through enjoying a relationship with Christ that has been examined and tested over time. Once trust is established, then we have faith that the relationship will continue with the same foundation of truth we recognized at the beginning. We learn we can continually depend upon God because, from the start, He has consistently proven himself to us and others.

Psalm 34:8 encourages us to "taste and see that the LORD is good." It is interesting, and awe-inspiring, that God requests action on our part, inviting us to look deeply into His character. The Lord is infinitely complex and leads us through a variety of individual experiences as we each work out our own unique fact-finding mission with Him.

In Conclusion

So resist the lie that Christians are not thinkers, that we are even anti-intellectual. Followers of Christ benefit when we assume a thoughtful, analytical mind-set, striving to free ourselves of prejudices or blinders. Even when approaching our spiritual life, the Lord has made it clear that He isn't looking for robots who automatically spew ideological theories that run no deeper than our metallic breastplates. Instead, He asks that we contemplatively:

- ❏ Remember that the wisdom of this world is foolishness in God's sight.
- ❏ Continue to work out our salvation with fear and trembling.
- ❏ Examine the Scriptures to confirm that what we hear is true.
- ❏ Test everything and hold on to the good.
- ❏ Watch our doctrine closely.
- ❏ Hold on in faith when God is silent.
- ❏ And taste and see that God is good.

Such contemplation prepares us to live in the intricate world where He has placed us. Whenever we enter into a discussion of the tough issues that sometimes divide our society, instead of throwing up the expected stone walls, let us do our best to break through barriers by taking on the mind of Christ. God gave us our incredible, complex minds. Let's use them for His glory.

About the Author: Cheryl Gochnauer is a homemaker and mother who maintains a web site for stay-at-home moms.

Common Misconception No. 3

Heard Outside the Church: "People like me would never be welcome in that church."

Heard Inside the Church: "We can't afford to accept just anyone into our church."

Background Scripture: 1 Samuel 16:7; Matthew 9:10-13; Luke 7:37-39; 19:1-10; John 3:16; Acts 10—11; Galatians 2:11-14; James 2:1-13; 2 Peter 3:9

CHAPTER 3

Christians Don't Like Anyone Who Is Different

by Darlene Teague

The sign on a church read: "Our Church Can Be Your Home."

What does such a sign imply about that church? About Christians in general? About how a nonbeliever might feel visiting that church? While this sign states that the congregation welcomes people into its family, it also implies there may be churches that do not feel like family.

So the question arises: Must Christians embrace all people, without regard to any conditions, in order to be perceived as tolerant of differences?

The View from Outside the Church

Some people think they just will not be comfortable in a church. Even if they don't see themselves as sinners, they know they do some things the church does not approve of. They figure that the church will let them know how different they are as soon as they walk in the door—and that won't be a very pleasant experience.

Perhaps they have had difficult encounters with church people before. Sadly, it is all too easy to find examples of people who, in the name of Christ, judge, criticize, reject, and ostracize others. Consequently, they would rather stay away from church than to take a chance that their past sins would be made a matter of public humiliation. And they do stay

away—unless someone shows them that the church will welcome them.

The View from Inside the Church

While most churches want new people to join them, it is
hard to know how to be accepting without being too tolerant.
The ideal is to "love the sinner and hate the sin," but how do
we accomplish that?

It is not easy, as the experience of one man shows. As an
editor for Sunday School materials, he regularly wrote editori-
als. Once he wrote an editorial titled "The Day I Smelled
Smoke in Church." He told about his reactions to smelling cig-
arette smoke on a person sitting in a nearby pew. At first, he
was appalled. "Nobody here smokes!" he thought. Then he re-
alized that this person was a visitor, and he needed to welcome him no matter how he smelled. The important thing was
that the visitor was in a place to hear the gospel preached.

When the editorial ran, the writer received some negative
mail. Some of his readers thought he was condoning smoking,
that he was lowering the Christian standards. They missed his
point entirely, but that is an easy thing to do. It is difficult to
know when welcoming ends and condoning begins.

Another concern arises in the church. Will having people
who are openly sinners come into the church weaken it?
Don't we need to protect our youth and new Christians from
bad influences? Some might wonder what would happen if
we invited the man from the office to church, knowing he
would bring his live-in girlfriend with him. Would that be
sending the wrong message to the singles in the congregation? To keep new Christians from becoming confused, don't
we need to guard the church from those people and ideas that
would taint it?

What's the Problem?

Why do some people think that Christians are intolerant?
Why are some Christians unable to separate welcoming from
condoning? It certainly can't be the gospel. We have a mes-

sage of love from God through Christ. Jesus told us to love others as He loved us. So, the message we preach and teach is not the problem.

Perhaps it is the way we *apply* the gospel we preach. We have a standard, a measuring rod, for determining right from wrong. It is God's Word. Within the community of faith, we accept God's Word as the final authority in issues of faith and life. And so we should. However, when we try to hold those outside the church to the principles of God's Word, they fall very short of Christian standards. Those outside the church feel our condemnation and think of us as narrow-minded.

We need to learn how to give sinners enough space, enough welcome, enough love that they will stay in the church long enough to be converted to Christ. We have no better place to learn how to do that than the New Testament we revere.

The View from the Bible

God has offered His grace to all people. He desires that every person would be in a right relationship with Him. John 3:16 says that God loved the world so much that He gave His Son for our salvation. There are no limitations in that verse, such as *"some* of the world," or *"most* of the world." He does not want anyone to perish. Rather He wants "everyone to come to repentance" (2 Peter 3:9).

We, as the Church, need to have God's perspective—salvation is for everyone. We must welcome all people as we offer Christ's gift of salvation, and depend on the fact that Christ will do whatever transforming they need.

While Jesus was on earth, He associated with people that the established religious authorities rejected. Luke 19:1-10 records the encounter Jesus had with the tax collector Zacchaeus. While the religious people shunned the wicked tax collector, Jesus offered him salvation. Zacchaeus wasn't the only tax collector with whom Jesus associated. Matthew 9:10-13 tells of at least one other time when Jesus ate with tax collectors and sinners.

On another occasion (Luke 7:37-39) when Jesus was in the home of a Pharisee, a woman who had lived a sinful life in that town came and washed Jesus' feet with her tears and dried them with her hair. The Pharisee said to himself that if Jesus were a prophet, He would know who was touching Him. Being touched by an unclean person was repulsive to the strict Jewish people. Jesus did know; still He offered her forgiveness for her sins.

After Jesus returned to heaven, it was up to His followers to spread the good news of salvation. However, it was difficult for them to go beyond the group they were most comfortable with—Jewish people. The early disciples had to struggle in order to overcome their idea that God's salvation was only for Jews.

Peter's experiences help us see how much effort it took to open the door of salvation to all people. Chapters 10 and 11 of the Book of Acts record the vision God gave to Peter concerning the Gentiles (that is, all persons who were not Jews). God instructed him not to call anything impure that He had made clean. Peter came to realize that "God does not show favoritism but accepts men from every nation who fear him and do what is right" (10:34-35).

Once Peter's eyes were opened, he had to help his fellow Jews see what God had shown him. He had to explain his actions to those who criticized him. Later, Peter had to relearn his lesson when Paul confronted him for being hypocritical. Galatians 2:11-14 recounts Paul's comments. Because Peter was afraid of those who were Jewish believers, he stopped eating with the Gentile Christians. Paul said that Peter was acting wrong in the way he treated his brothers in Christ. Could it be that sometimes we treat people improperly because of fear of what our friends will think?

Jesus' brother, James, gave specific instructions about this matter. James 2:1-13 says that we sin when we show favoritism. In James's day (as it is in ours), it was easy to prefer one person over another because of appearance, possessions, or position. However, as God said to Samuel concerning human opinions, "The LORD does not look at the things man looks at. Man looks at the outward appearance, but the LORD looks at the heart" (1 Samuel 16:7).

A poorly dressed man came into a church one Sunday morning. The pews were filled; there was not a place for him to sit. He walked to the front of the sanctuary and sat on the floor. The people in the pews looked at him in surprise (some in shock!). Didn't he know that people do not go sit on the floor in church—especially up front?

One of the older men of the church got up from his seat and went to the man. Folks looked at each other knowingly. He would straighten out the guy. Instead, without saying a word, the older man sat on the floor beside the newcomer.

The Right Perspective

When sinners are brave enough to risk a visit to church, we can break down the barriers that make Christians seem intolerant. First, we can accept them where they are spiritually when they come into our congregation. We can embrace them in love, no matter how they smell or look. Then we can live, preach, and teach the truth of the gospel. There is no need to lower our standards. And they will feel free to stay and we will be available to help as the Holy Spirit does His transforming work in their lives.

The following true story from a Sunday School teacher shows how this can happen even with people most unlikely to be good prospects for the church.

Roy spent his evenings and weekends at the local nightclubs and bars, drinking, dancing, and having a good time. His bad temper caused more than one barroom brawl.

He had gone through a bitter divorce and was lonely. He could forget his troubles and loneliness in the party atmosphere and loud music of the beer joints.

That's where he met Mary. She was also divorced, lonely, and hurting. At first, they were just friends, then they became a couple, and Mary moved in with Roy. They both loved to dance and continued to frequent the bars, looking for excitement and fulfillment in their lives.

One evening after they had returned home from the bar, Roy told Mary that he wanted to ask her a very important question. He asked her to give it careful thought before she answered.

She noticed that he had been very quiet all evening. Puzzled at his somber tone, she sat on a chair. Roy kneeled in front of her, gently took her hand, and smiled. "Mary, will you marry me?"

Tears stung her eyes as she nodded yes. As they embraced, Roy further surprised her when he whispered in her ear, "Let's make some changes in our life and have a church wedding." Mary responded that she would like that very much.

As they made plans, she recalled that when she was a young girl, she had attended a local church a few times with one of her neighbors. Roy looked thoughtful for a minute and said, "You know, when I was a boy, I sometimes used to ride the church bus to that same church."

"It's settled then," Mary agreed. She called the pastor, and he agreed to talk with them about their wedding.

They were greeted warmly and spent about an hour visiting with the pastor. He agreed to marry them if they would come in each week for counseling for the next three months. He also surprised them when he suggested that they live apart during those three months. Then, if they still wanted to get married, he would marry them.

At first, they were shocked at his suggestion; but as the pastor talked with them about marriage as God had ordained it, they agreed.

Before they left, the pastor suggested that, in order to get their lives back in the right perspective, they should also read their Bibles and attend church regularly. It didn't have to be his church, but he assured them they would be welcome there. Because of his influence, they were soon attending his Sunday School and church regularly.

True to their promise, Roy and Mary lived apart for three months and were married in the church.

Roy and Mary's spiritual development was slow. At times, they seemed to argue a lot. They enrolled in the church's marriage enrichment class and, at first, even bickered a little in the class sessions.

Mary began showing spiritual growth, but Roy seemed to lag behind. "He just needs some more time to grow in his faith. Be patient with him," the pastor advised us.

We invited him to join our church softball team. As we got to know him, we found him to be likable and friendly. Roy also began attending our men's meetings on a regular basis.

It was a day of great rejoicing when, about six months after their wedding, Roy and Mary accepted Jesus Christ as their Savior.

It's been several years now, and Roy and Mary have proven that they are very serious about living their lives for Christ. Both serve in leadership positions in the church. They teach an adult Sunday School class, and she serves as missionary society president. Roy was recently elected to be on the church board.

Mary and Roy just prove that church prospects are everywhere—even nightclubs and bars.*

Welcome Home

Home is the place that everyone needs to be able to return and find a welcome. The church needs to be a home where sinners can come and find salvation for their sin-sick souls. Those of us already inside the church need not fear that sinners coming into our midst will weaken our witness. In fact, that is what the church is for—the conversion of sinners. How will they be converted if they never feel welcome enough to come home? And we can rest assured that God will help us find the balance we need as we love and accept people *and* keep a biblical stand against sin.

---

*"Unlikely Church Prospects," © 2001 by Joe Seay. Used by permission. All rights reserved.

About the Author: Darlene Teague is an editor of curriculum materials for The Wesleyan Church in Indianapolis.

Common Misconception No. 4

Heard Outside the Church: "Everyone must find his or her own way to God, however possible."

Heard Inside the Church: "God is too loving to send anyone to hell."

Background Scripture: Psalm 118:22; Matthew 7:13-20; 28:18-20; John 10:7-9; 14:6; Acts 4:11-12; 11:26; 17:16-34; 19:9, 23; 24:14, 22; Romans 2:14-15; Hebrews 11

CHAPTER 4

All Religions Are Equally Good

by Joseph E. Coleson

"All paths lead to the top of the mountain." Ever heard that line? It is fairly common today when people are talking about the eternal destiny of human beings, though certainly it is expressed more often by non-Christians than by Christians.

So, do all paths really lead to the top of the mountain? One could, in theory, ascend to the summit of any literal mountain by any route up any of its slopes. But I have had just enough experience climbing mountains to know that, in practice, it's not that easy. Some mountain slopes can (and do) kill any average climber foolhardy enough to attempt them. Even skilled and experienced climbers have conquered some "impossible" routes only at great risk. Taken literally, this common saying is a dangerous one.

This adage is, of course, a metaphor. It refers, not to a literal mountain, but to eternal life in heaven with God. Its intent is not to suggest that only the spiritually skilled and experienced will reach heaven. Just the opposite is meant; this proverb suggests the vast majority of humans will reach heaven, no matter what path they follow to that desirable destination. It suggests that heaven is only a mile-high summit, and all its approaches are gentle, paved, and easy inclines, with frequent rest stops.

Yet, not every metaphor fits. This one asserts that every religion (or no religion at all) is equally certain to bring one at the end of life to heaven. After all, God is benevolent and "too good and loving to send anyone to hell" (which is the com-

mon way even some Christians express this idea). The question is, does this metaphor fit? Does it present an accurate picture of everyone's eternal destiny?

The answer is vital. Wishing does not make something
true, nor does expressing it as a pleasant-sounding metaphor.
If God truly exists, as Christians believe, then Christians at
least need to discover what God has to say on the subject. The
Bible reveals God's view quite clearly, and the Church generally has been consistent in its interpretation and teaching of
what the Bible presents.

Jesus Called Himself the Way

The Bible declares, and the Christian faith in all its true
forms has accepted, that God made a way to heaven for the
human race; and, in fact, that Way is Jesus. Furthermore, Jesus is the *only* Way. Jesus himself, speaking to Thomas and
the other disciples in the Upper Room the evening before He
was crucified, said, "I am the Way and the Truth and the Life;
no one comes to the Father if not through Me" (John 14:6).[1]

A word about right and wrong methods of interpreting
the Bible: If the Bible is God's revelation, it will not contradict
its own *verifiable* teaching; and if it seems to, we must look for
and find a better understanding. Thus, if this were the only
passage stating or implying that one can come to God only
through Jesus, and if other passages stated or implied that
(many) other ways to God exist, then we would have to find
another meaning for Jesus' words here, or show that Jesus did
not really say them, or did not mean them as the Church his-
torically has understood them.

However, this most definitely is *not* the only biblical
statement that God has provided the definitive path to heav-
en in the person of Jesus Christ. It would take many chapters
to explore fully all the ways in which God's promise of redemption is stated again and again in the pages of the Old
Testament, and the means by which God prepared Israel and
the world for the coming of the Redeemer. So high were the
expectations of the Jewish people of the Holy Land in the first
century that they followed several charismatic leaders who

promised to deliver them from the rule of Rome. Those expectations were not wrong, but God's program of redemption was far greater than they imagined. Many missed the true Redeemer because He did not act as they expected Him to act. Many followed false redeemers to their destruction.

Tutored by the Holy Spirit to recall Jesus' teachings and their true significance, the apostles and the rest of the Early Church proclaimed the good news that God has indeed provided a Way to heaven. They were clear in their witness that this Way was and is Jesus himself, the Messiah (in Hebrew), the Christ (in Greek).

Matthew recorded Jesus' own teaching about the broad and the narrow ways most clearly in the climactic section of the Sermon on the Mount (7:13-20). In this passage, Jesus did not explicitly identify himself as the gate or the road but prepared His hearers for that later revelation by His authoritative emphasis that, in fact, the small gate and the narrow road are not found by all. To "find" in this context does not mean to discover as though one never had heard of this before, but to accept that, in fact, this small gate and narrow road are *the* Way provided by God for those who would enter eternal life. To find means to accept, if one's chosen destination is heaven, that this is the Gate one must enter, and this Way leads there. In a similar vein on another occasion, Jesus made this idea more explicit and clear when He called himself the Door, not once, but twice (John 10:7, 9).[2]

By contrast, the wide gate and the broad way of Matthew 7:13 signal lack of direction; lack of purpose; lack of understanding and faith; aimlessness, as opposed to moving toward a goal. Nevertheless, mere motion does not save. Jesus is the Redeemer, and He did the work that accomplished our redemption. However, moving along the narrow way is a good indicator of being in right relationship with God. Where God is, God's people want to be. If the narrow way is the way to God, God's people want to be on it.

Jesus Commissioned Us to Teach That He Is the Way

Jesus' Great Commission, given just before His ascension (recorded in Matthew 28:18-20), is another indication that He attached great importance to people knowing Him as the Way. Jesus began with an amazing statement: "All authority has been given to Me in heaven and upon earth" (v. 18). If Jesus was not what the Scriptures proclaim Him to be—what He himself claimed to be—then He was, at best, a deluded, eccentric, but harmless madman; at worst, He was a raving, lying, dangerous megalomaniac. But if this statement is true, then Jesus is what He claimed to be, and that includes being the only Way. As many have observed, there is no middle ground, no basis for taking Jesus as just one of many good teachers in the world's history.

If Jesus possesses all authority, it follows that no other way could be valid unless Jesus should validate it. His instruction, as expressed in the Great Commission, indicates that He did not endorse any other way. Rather, Jesus' followers are to dedicate their lives to informing everyone that *He* is the Way.

"Go, therefore [*because* all authority is given to Me], and disciple all the peoples" (v. 19). What does "disciple" mean? It means "baptizing them in the name of the Father and of the Son and of the Holy Spirit" (v. 19), that is, into identity as part of the family of God through faith in Jesus as the Way. It also means "teaching them to attend to all that I have commanded you" (v. 20), that is, to follow Jesus as the Way, to walk as He both showed and instructed us to walk. In the earliest years, Christians even were known as the people of *the Way*. See Acts 19:9, 23 and 24:14, 22.

The Early Church Understood That Jesus Is the Only Way

Peter and Paul were two of the most important leaders and teachers of the Early Church, as indicated by the New Testament record. Both these men were emphatic that Jesus was and is the Way God has given the human race to gain access to God and heaven.

Very early in the Church's history, before Paul had become a Christian, before the Church even had spread beyond

Jerusalem, Peter—quoting Psalm 118:22—declared Jesus "the Stone . . . which became the Cornerstone" (Acts 4:11). Peter went on to define Jesus' role as the Cornerstone more precisely and emphatically: "And there is not salvation in any other, for there is *no other* name under heaven given among human beings by which it is necessary that we may be saved" (v. 12, emphasis added). In other words, if we are going to be saved from the death we all experience because of human alienation from God, no one else but Jesus can do it.

A few years later Paul, having become the leading evangelist to non-Jews, spoke to Athenian philosophers who had not yet heard of Jesus (Acts 17:16-34). Paul gained their attention by quoting their own poets and noting the dedication of one of the many idol altars in the center of Athens, "TO AN UNKNOWN GOD." That, Paul said, is the God of whom he was speaking. Paul spent most of his brief speech disclosing the One whom we would call today the First Person of the Trinity. But his conclusion, and the climax toward which he moved his address, was the assertion that God's plan for the culmination of the world's history centered in the person and redemptive work of Jesus. Jesus was not just *a* way, but God's chosen Way to attain the righteousness for which we have longed ever since that ancient day in the garden when first we forsook it.

Today, obviously, most people outside the Church do not believe this. Even within the Church, many people are willing to believe that Jesus is a good Way for Western Christians, but not necessarily the only Way for all people around the world. Still, the Early Church and the whole New Testament were not vague on this point. Certainly Peter, Paul, and the rest of the Early Church believed Jesus was God's appointed—and *only*—Way to eternal life with God in heaven.

Who Gets to Heaven?

Who, then, gets to go to heaven, and how do they get there? For clarity's sake, we first must address another question, briefly: "What is a Christian?"

Since the term "Christian" was first used in Antioch (Acts 11:26), it follows that God's people before Jesus could not have been "Christians." Are they in heaven? The Bible clearly teaches that Jesus died for the believers who lived before He came to earth, as well as for those who lived after. As we see in Hebrews 11, all persons of faith who had gone before focused their faith on God's promises. The fulfillment of God's promises to them has now come in Jesus Christ, and their redemption, too, is now complete in Him. Thus, they are in heaven.

Most Christians have believed that infants and children, too, if they die before the age when they can understand and accept Jesus as their own Savior and Lord, are in heaven. At least these two groups of people, who cannot be called "Christian" in a personal sense, will be in heaven.

It gets a little more complicated from here. As the Christian faith spread around the world and down the ages to the present, "Christian" has become a cultural, but not necessarily religious, identifier in some places.

In predominantly Muslim Arab countries, Christians are those whose ancestors through the centuries did not convert to the Muslim faith after the Muslim conquests of the seventh century. In Israel, "Christian" includes almost anyone who is not Jewish or Muslim. The Philippines is a largely Christian country, and most Christians are Catholic. There, "born again" refers to any Christian who is not Catholic. In the United States, however, many who call themselves "born again" do not consider anyone Christian unless they, too, would describe themselves as "born again."

And what of Paul's teaching in Romans 2, that those who have not heard "law" (Torah, instruction) yet may be judged righteous by God if they do "by nature" "the things of the Torah" (v. 14)? It would seem to be possible—not probable, but possible—that some persons do seek after God consistently, living by the best light their culture can give, so that their "thoughts" may "defend" them (v. 15).

This is not to say, however, that any path will bring us to the top of the mountain. If we follow on with our metaphor, we should say, rather, that God graces such seekers so that they find the Way, even though circumstances of their history and geography prevent them from ever hearing the name of the Way. It may happen in God's grace and providence, but not often enough that Christians should depend on it for the lives of those who never have heard. We still are charged with the Great Commission. We still affirm that "there is no other name under heaven given to men by which we must be saved" (Acts 4:12, NIV).

A Final Thought

We miss the mark if and when we think of heaven as some ultimate prize found by the diligent or the fortunate few, who then may be viewed, somehow, as "deserving." The Bible teaches, and Wesleyanism at its best always has stressed, that heaven is only heaven because God is there. We seek not a place, but a relationship with God. Jesus is God. To reject Jesus is to reject God and any relationship with God.

Jesus is the only Way not because God arbitrarily arranged things so that the greatest possible number of people could be kept out of His heaven. Jesus is the only Way because only Jesus is God. Knowing Moses, or Socrates, or Plato, or the Dalai Lama, may be very good things, but knowing any other good teacher is not the same as knowing Jesus, any more than knowing the governor of your state or province means you know the president or the prime minister.

God is a Person—or three Persons in One, to be precise. It is not unreasonable to find that if one wishes to know the Father, one needs to be introduced by the Son.

Notes:
1. Unless indicated, all translations are the author's. Some are a bit wooden, to bring out the emphasis of the original language.
2. The NIV translates this as "gate" rather than "door."

About the Author: Dr. Coleson is professor of Hebrew Scriptures at Nazarene Theological Seminary, Kansas City.

Common Misconception No. 5

Heard Outside the Church: "How can Christians tell anyone anything when they can't agree among themselves?"

Heard Inside the Church: "I may have to love my Christian brothers and sisters, but I don't have to like them."

Background Scripture: John 17:11, 20-21; 1 Corinthians 12:12-20; Ephesians 4:4-6

CHAPTER 5

Christians Can't Agree on Anything

by David W. Holdren

The headline read: "Orthodox Priests in Fistfight with Franciscan Monks at Church of the Nativity."

For some, the first reaction would be, "No way!" Monks and priests fighting? It doesn't happen!

However, others would say, "See, even the very religious can't get along!"

Which is your response?

Actually, the headline could have appeared in any newspaper in the late 1800s. The two groups, the Greek Orthodox Church and the Franciscan order of the Roman Catholic Church, have both claimed that the Church of the Nativity—the traditional site of Jesus' birth—is their property. The contention got so out of hand in the 19th century that violent clashes broke out between the two groups. From 1873 until the present day, policemen have patrolled the church so that no more fistfights will occur.

Such a violent example of disagreement raises an important question. Those outside the church wag their heads and ask, "Can't Christians agree on anything?" Those inside the church repeat the plaintive cry, "Can't we just all get along?"

Outside, Looking In

People who don't understand Christianity point to churches on every corner and wonder why there are so many denominations. In their view, this group of Christians doesn't get along with that group, so they go off and start a different denomination. This has been repeated so often there are literally thousands of Christian denominations.

One fellow claimed that he had gone down the street in a very small town and found only two churches, sitting directly opposite one another at a street intersection. One church's sign read: "First Baptist Church." The other church's sign said: "Trine-immersion, Fire-baptized, Free-will, True Church of God Baptist Church."

The man jokingly commented, "They definitely have had a theological discussion in that town."

That's how church divisions appear to those looking in from the outside of Christianity.

How It Looks Inside

Sometimes it doesn't look much better to those who have been Christians a long time. Sometimes it looks like a jumble of theological confusion.

Take the important matter of salvation. Most Christians agree that salvation through Christ is the most important aspect of faith. But ask them how we "get" this salvation, and then stand back! Strict Calvinists claim that God has already determined every person's eternal destiny—heaven or hell—by what is called "predestination." The Wesleyan-Holiness crowd claim that salvation is simply and only by faith.

Such emphasis on the differences between denominations causes us to lose sight of a very important idea: Each denomination has a particular purpose. Each has been raised up to highlight a particular part of the Christian mission. One way to think of it is to imagine that Christianity is a large, multifaceted jewel. As we hold that precious stone up and slowly turn it, we see different patterns as the light shines through it. Yet, it is one gem. Denominational distinctives are like the facets of the jewel, each adding its own dimension to the total beauty.

Disagreeable Results

These perceptions about disagreement within Christiani-

ty have some detrimental effects. Seeing so many denominations causes many to be confused about Christianity. If Christians disagree so much, they wonder if they can believe anything Christians say. People who are seriously searching for
spiritual answers wander off to other religions, no longer
willing to look to Christianity for answers.

Within the Church, disagreement in its mild form results
in isolation. Various Christian groups stay in their own little
worlds, never interacting with each other. There is no fellowship among different groups of believers and little appreciation for each other's spiritual gifts.

In its worst forms, disagreement causes outright fights,
like the ones between the monks and the priests at the Church
of the Nativity. However, it happens in the middle of congregations as well. And congregational civil war is a killer. We
have seen it for years. Power struggles and carnal attitudes of
criticism, gossip, and lack of forgiveness demolish the witness
of a group to the church community, its children, and the
community around them.

Out of frustration, many Christians give up trying to
find their way through this theological maze. They then say
things like, "I have to love my fellow Christians, but I don't
have to like them!"

What's the Answer?

We are different; it's a human thing. We have differences
in *personality*. Our past *experiences* and the *cultures* in which
we were raised reveal many variations among us. *Ethnicity*,
language, and *color* are different features nearly impossible to
change. God made us *male* and *female*, a very noticeable distinction. Of course, we also find differences in *values* and *priorities* among the variety of mortals.

There is nothing necessarily wrong or bad about our
many differences. It is what we do with our differences and
how they affect us, our relationships, and our influence that
brings concern.

Have you ever listened, enraptured, to a piano being

played beautifully? Every key on a piano is different from all the others; each has its own tone. Yet, when differing keys are played in proper relationship to each other, an amazing thing occurs—harmonious chords. On the other hand, if each note is struck in competition with the others, an awful sound occurs—discord, or just plain noise. Unity within diversity is called harmony, and that is the answer to our disagreements. Harmony is a beautiful thing to hear in music, and it is lovely to behold in relationships.

Now, we can see why one of Christ's greatest desires for His followers is for unity. Listen to the intimate and passionate appeal of our Savior as He prayed: "Holy Father, protect them . . . that they may be one as we are one. . . . I pray also for those who will believe . . . that all of them may be *one* . . . so that the world may believe that you have sent me" (John 17:11, 20-21, emphasis added).

Why was Jesus so passionate about unity among His followers? Because of the positive power unity would have on those who were watching and who needed to come to Him in faith for salvation.

The apostle Paul, one of the earliest and most famous Christians, helps us see further the unity for which Christ prayed. He talks about the *importance of our differences.* If we let our differences become compliments (and complements) rather than criticisms, everybody wins. If we realize that we truly do need each other because of our own deficiencies and imperfections, we all have reason to feel better about ourselves and each other.

Here's how Paul explains it in 1 Corinthians 12:12-20. He helps us look at any given collection of Christians as if they are a body—a spiritual yet literal body, with each person being a different but contributing part. He tells us not to diminish our own contribution, or to be jealous of another and his or her strength and contribution. In essence, he says that in the Church of Jesus Christ, everybody is somebody special. By the grace of God, we need to learn to take our differences and transform them into contributions and compliments, rather than conflicts and criticisms.

Paul also reminds us of *the power of things that we have in common*—values, experiences, and sources that draw us together. Though some of the sources of unity in secular arenas of life include a common enemy, common good, common sources, or common passions and goals, he referred to what Christians have in common: "One body . . . one Spirit . . . called to one hope . . . one Lord, one faith, one baptism; one God and Father of all" (Ephesians 4:4-6). So we must let those points of unity become stronger than our differences and the attitudes that divide us.

The Great Power in Unity

I can easily remember my amazement as a seven-year-old kid at the power of a magnifying glass. While its primary purpose for Grandpa was to help him read the newspaper, it was a fascination for me. I could take mildly warm rays of sun and focus them through that special lens on a piece of paper or a dry leaf. What was merely warm became a laser beam of heat, then a flame, as the result of the focused energy.

Hatred and love, division and unity—each and all have great power when they are focused. On which will we focus?

The power of unity is experienced in *impact*. That impact may be in terms of victory or blessing. Even the "bad guys" of the world experience victory when through a concentration of unity they conquer some challenge. And so can unity be the catalyst for impact for Christ.

The power of unity is experienced in *celebration*. Whenever unity prevails, even without other so-called results or accomplishments, it nearly always fosters a sense of celebration and joy. It has its own pure power that just seems good and right for those who experience it. It's like a foretaste of heaven.

The power of unity is experienced in *community*. Along with celebration comes a beautiful and wonderful bond. The Bible uses a term, *koinonia*, that means deep and transforming togetherness and a bond that dignifies and strengthens those who share it. The sweet sense of belonging and being valued among a group is a prized experience when unity prevails.

The power of unity is experienced through *witness*. That was the longing Jesus had when He prayed to the Heavenly Father for our unity as His followers "that the world may believe" (John 17:21).

The power of unity is experienced by Christ as *honor*. That's right. Maybe the most important power of unity is what it means to our Creator and Savior. It is honoring to God. When we gather for what we call "corporate worship," it is not about some corporation worshiping. It is about a gathering of people who have multitudes of differences, yet come together to praise and honor God, to seek His grace and guidance in each one of the lives present.

New Breezes of Unity Are Blowing

It is easy enough to focus on the differences between religions, denominations, and even within congregations. There is ample history to review on that issue. We can spend all our time trying to prove how we're different from all the others.

However, there is a clear and exciting new inclination for Christians of all "brands" to see how our denominational distinctives can work together to accomplish the Great Commission. When that occurs, our differences are neither the cause of discord and division nor blended into a bland, generic Christianity. Rather, as each denomination lends its distinction to a harmonious unity, we move closer to accomplishing God's purpose for humanity—namely, that every person come to a saving knowledge of Jesus Christ.

A new day is dawning in which we can stop grappling over our differences and begin focusing on our oneness in Christ. It is a day when we can respond to God's call by building bridges rather than erecting fences. Even when it comes to our relationship with the world "out there" beyond the church, we can do a better job of winning them to Christ if we can live out our unity among diversity.

Taking all differences into consideration, a growing passion exists among Christian groups to focus on our being commonly blessed *through* Christ, so we can together be a blessing *for* Christ. It is an exciting thing to see Christians coming together in prayer for spiritual awakening among our communities and nations.

About the Author: Dr. Holdren is a general superintendent of The Wesleyan Church.

Common Misconception No. 6

Heard Outside the Church: "The Bible is just a human book and is irrelevant to real life."

Heard Inside the Church: "The old standards don't apply anymore."

Background Scripture: Judges 17:6; Psalm 19:7-11; Matthew 5:17-19; 2 Timothy 3:16-17

CHAPTER 6

Absolutely No Absolutes!

by Kevin D. Newburg

The Bible isn't reluctant to come right out and proclaim its importance. "All Scripture is God-breathed and is useful for teaching, rebuking, correcting and training in righteousness, so that the man of God may be thoroughly equipped for every good work" (2 Timothy 3:16-17).

However, the skeptic takes immediate exception. "There are lots of great books out there. Certainly the Bible would have to be considered one of them. However, just as you wouldn't orient your life around the writings of Shakespeare, Dickens, or Twain, neither should people use the Bible as an 'instruction book' for life. It's just a book, written by normal people who were trying to make sense of their world. It's an ancient book. And while it has some interesting stories and provides us with some historical information, it shouldn't be used as the ultimate guide for life. In fact, nothing should take on that role universally. No one can say what's right and wrong for someone else. The shoulds and should-nots, oughts and ought-nots, of my life are mine, and I shouldn't try to impose them on you."

Individual Freedom

And so the argument goes: *the only absolute is that there are no absolutes.* Truth and reality are perceived as ambiguous. Meaning is determined by the individual at the moment. Each life is so different from every other that no one could ever truly understand what someone else is experiencing or feeling.

My story is mine, your story is yours; they are independent and unique. There are no overriding principles, no universal ethics, no real standards by which to judge or evaluate. Ultimately this philosophy argues that society cannot judge the acceptability of any form of expression, any standard, any lifestyle. The strongest statement one can make is, "It's not for me. But as long as no one is hurt, who can object?"

The Bible has a different view. This isn't the first time such a situation has existed. It was a popular idea early in history. "In those days Israel had no king; everyone did as he saw fit" (Judges 17:6).

Christian Individuality

We have come now to believe that *individual* freedom is the basis of democracy. Individual rights have become the ultimate goal, which must always be defended. Therefore, I have no right to tell you how you should live. As long as no one else's individual rights are abused, you should have the freedom to do whatever you want to do. That's what makes our country "great."

We equate the principles on which our country is founded as Christian principles. Then we also equate democracy with Christianity. We associate our nation so closely with Christianity that we reason backward that individual liberty is a Christian belief. It's a small step from individual rights to the absence of moral absolutes. Therefore, the Church has no right to tell anyone what is right or wrong, which would equal the denial of individual liberty.

Within the Church, the same philosophy is encountered in a variety of ways. The Christian businessperson argues, "No harm, no foul. It's a dog-eat-dog world out there. 'Every man for himself.' The law says you must do it a certain way, but everyone knows nobody does it that way. Besides, the only reason they made that rule was to make us pay more taxes. If we don't cut corners, somebody else will underbid us, and then where will our company be? What will happen to our employees then?"

In the absence of absolutes, and surrounded by coworkers and competitors who either subtly or blatantly avoid, compromise, or reinterpret what's acceptable, it becomes difficult for some Christians to practice Christianity at work. Sometimes there are pressures to go along. At times those pressures can be severe—the threatened loss of a job, for example. It can, over time, cause us to not even recognize that what we're doing is wrong. Not wrong because we might get caught. Not wrong because we're ripping off the company. Not wrong because we're circumventing the law. But wrong because it's just plain wrong.

"And they brought to Jesus a man who had been caught stealing from his company. And Jesus said to them, 'Have you not eyes to see and ears to hear? His company took unfair advantage of him. He wasn't paid enough. Nobody was really hurt. And everyone else in his office was doing it. This man is a good man. He loves his wife, tolerates his children, goes to church most of the time. You Pharisees, with your rules, lighten up! Ease off! Get real! You cannot expect a man to be perfect at work.' And the man went away feeling much better about himself."

Never heard that version of Scripture, have you? And you never will, because Jesus would never compromise the truth.

Individualistic Choices

Still, in a modern world that seems devoid of absolutes, that is filled with personal interpretations, each of which is claimed to be as valid as any other, it's easy to say: "The movie wasn't all that bad." "The song has a nice tune, though the words are rather suggestive." "Sure, alcoholism is a serious problem, but there's nothing wrong with a cold beer on a hot afternoon." "The TV show's characters don't have very good morals, but they are really funny."

If we don't believe in absolutes, then it really isn't very important that we know just what we do believe. We won't say one religion has it "right," and another has it "wrong." If it's all a matter of opinion, and every opinion or interpretation is as good as another, then all these theological nuances are just a nuisance.

Sadly then, Christian distinctives and guidelines are accepted or rejected based primarily on personal convenience. What a contrast with the attitude of John Wesley, who we can paraphrase. "If it doesn't strengthen your relationship with God, if instead by hearing, seeing, reading, or watching, your relationship with God is even in a small way weakened, avoid that thing."*

This Isn't the Old Days

Long gone are the Wesleyan accountability groups. In them, individuals openly confessed to a half dozen other Christians what they did, said, and thought or failed to do or say. Then they asked for help in discerning whether their action was right or wrong, whether or not they had sinned. They allowed the group to hold them accountable in the future. Such a group is a completely foreign notion to many today.

Accountability, rules, absolutes are all rejected as old-fashioned, antiquated, the remnant of a belief system based more on the Old Testament than on the teachings of Jesus. One person says, "You know, all the 'thou shalts' are in the Old Testament. Jesus never talked like that. In fact, it seems that Jesus really came to correct the inadequate teachings of the Old Testament." Another speaks for many others, "The Old Testament doesn't make sense to me." Or some Christians say, "I enjoy reading the Gospels. I like the things Jesus says. Jesus talks about freedom and love, joy and happiness. The God in the Old Testament seems to be so angry. Jesus isn't into all those rules."

Yet Jesus said:

> Do not think that I have come to abolish the Law or the Prophets; I have not come to abolish them but to fulfill them. I tell you the truth, until heaven and earth disappear, not the smallest letter, not the least stroke of a pen, will by any means disappear from the Law until every-

thing is accomplished. Anyone who breaks one of the least of these commandments and teaches others to do the same will be called least in the kingdom of heaven, but whoever practices and teaches these commands will be called great in the kingdom of heaven *(Matthew 5:17-19)*.

Jesus' teaching and ministry is built on the foundation of the Old Testament. Yet, in a culture where we try to avoid absolutes, where we don't believe in absolutes, the Old Testament makes us very uncomfortable. Not simply for its lists of dos and don'ts, but also because it is filled with stories of people who disregard those injunctions and end up facing very serious consequences. It's much easier to dismiss them as old-fashioned, irrelevant, superseded, or optional than it is to accept these stories as foundational.

We Need Rules

The Bible isn't reluctant to come right out and tell us how to live, and rightly so.

The law of the LORD is perfect, reviving the soul. The statutes of the LORD are trustworthy, making wise the simple. The precepts of the LORD are right, giving joy to the heart. The commands of the LORD are radiant, giving light to the eyes. The fear of the LORD is pure, enduring forever. The ordinances of the LORD are sure and altogether righteous. They are more precious than gold, than much pure gold; they are sweeter than honey, than honey from the comb. By them is your servant warned; in keeping them there is great reward *(Psalm 19:7-11)*.

The absence of rules is chaos. What a mess we would have if everyone ignored stop signs, decided not to pay for their groceries, or chose not to work while still expecting a salary. We readily acknowledge the need for and accept the presence of rules in our lives. Yet even within the Church, we are tempted to be coerced by a culture that asserts that those rules shouldn't apply to personal ethics; that the traditional Christian concept of sin is antiquated and irrelevant.

Still, it is as important that we understand our faith and

heritage as it is that we understand the rules of the road. There are ethical absolutes. There are activities that are always wrong. There are responsibilities we cannot avoid. But they are not heavy burdens we cannot bear, or rules that rob our lives of joy. Rather, they free us up to fully follow God, and that is true freedom—absolutely!

Note:

*Wesley's actual words were: "One design you are to pursue to the end of time, the enjoyment of God in time and in eternity. Desire other things, so far as they tend to this. Love the creature as it leads to the Creator. But in every step you take, be this the glorious point that terminates your view. Let every affection, and thought, and word, and work, be subordinate to this" (*The Complete Works of John Wesley*, vol. 5, *Sermons* [Albany, Oreg.: AGES Software, 1997], 288).

About the Author: Kevin Newburg is senior pastor of the First Church of the Nazarene, Tacoma, Washington.

Common Misconception No. 7

Heard Outside the Church: "All Christians think the same way, vote the same way, and even try to look and act alike."

Heard Inside the Church: "Christians are supposed to think the same way, vote the same way, and act alike."

Background Scripture: Mark 3:17; 10:43-45; Acts 2:8-11; 6:1; 15:1-29, 36-41; 1 Corinthians 1:2, 5, 7; Galatians 2:11-14; Ephesians 4:4-6, 7

CHAPTER 7

All Christians Are Alike

by C. S. Cowles

She sat slumped down on the front row in class. Staring at the floor. Never taking a note. And doing poorly on her quizzes and exams.

Knowing that her father was a struggling pastor, I became increasingly annoyed at her obvious disinterest. She didn't seem to be trying. I thought of all kinds of ways to describe her, including "poor student," "lazy," "slacker," and even "non-Christian."

One day I asked her to remain after class. "Do you realize that you are failing?" I asked, barely disguising my irritation.

"Yes," she responded, with downcast eyes.

"I can't help but notice that you seem totally disengaged. I've never seen you take one note."

With a look of panic in her eyes, she nearly screamed, "I can't see!"

I sat in stunned silence as she explained that she couldn't see out of her left eye at all, and that everything was just a blur in her right eye. That's why she wasn't taking notes. And she had not been able to read her textbook and was, of course, doing poorly in class.

A battery of tests by an ophthalmologist had ruled out brain tumors, and she had an appointment that week to see a neurologist. Shaken by this disclosure, I prayed with her and offered to walk with her in the days ahead. Several weeks later, she shared with me the physician's diagnosis: multiple sclerosis. Its first symptom, in her case, was an attack on the optic nerves.

I was utterly embarrassed, chagrined, and ashamed for assuming that she was sloughing off in class when she actually was undergoing the most difficult crisis of her life. The labels that had gone through my head had not defined the reality of the situation. Really, I had *mis*labeled her.

Labeling is like putting a title on that drawer that contains all the clutter, such as batteries, string, scissors, crayons, paper clips, electric cords, and so on. At home, we call it the "junk drawer." Not that its contents are junk. We just refuse to make an enormous label to describe everything it contains. While labels are helpful to distinguish one item from another, they can be misleading when placed on people or movements. Yet we are prone to stick them on persons without the facts that come from close scrutiny.

Once again, I was reminded of the perils of prejudging and making sweeping generalizations about people, especially the description of Christians as all alike. Nevertheless, since such characterizations do contain an element of truth and are believed to be true by those who hold such opinions, we must unpack them in the light of the Word of God and the experience of the Church.

Uniformity

There is truth in the charge, "All Christians think the same way, vote the same way, and even try to look and act alike." Not only for Christians, but for everybody in general and each social group in particular, we are far more alike than different. It is not likely that a human being will be confused with a crocodile or a peregrine falcon.

Within the human species there are physical and cultural characteristics that define us according to races, nationalities, and, in many cases, religions. Few would mistake a Catholic priest for a rock star. All social groups, small and large, reflect common ways they speak, dress, and act that set them apart from other social groups. All we have to do is hear someone speak, and we can tell whether they grew up in Boston or Houston or France. Farmers tend to vote one way, and urban dwellers another.

So we should not be surprised that what sociologists call "the principle of homogeneity" is reflected in churches. Even as from the moment of birth we automatically adopt the language, customs, and values of our immediate family, it ought not to be surprising that we embrace their religious and political views as well. Children born and raised in Mormon homes grow up to become Mormons, and those from Jewish families Jews. No matter how energetically young people may try to distance themselves from their roots, they seldom ever completely escape the deep imprint of their early family and culture. A kind of groupthink and "group look" is inevitable whenever people gather together for any length of time.

Nevertheless, Christians are no more cookie-cutter in look, behavior, and tastes than motorcycle riders, police officers, or politicians. Beneath the appearance of sameness are also vast differences.

Diversity

While every human being shares the same average body temperature, there are no two with identical fingerprints or personalities or opinions. What is truly amazing, when we get beyond surface appearances, is not that Christians are so alike but that they are so different. So different that one wonders at times how they manage to worship in the same congregation and belong to the same denomination. Often, of course, they do not. The disputes become so rancorous that they go their separate ways. The very fact that there are currently more than 33,000 different Christian denominations, sects, and cults in the world attests to this. Even within a given denomination or local congregation, the diversity of theological and political opinions is truly surprising.

We don't have to look any further than Jesus' tight band of disciples to see diversity on full display. True, they shared some things in common: all were Jews, none were of the priestly or ruling class, and all had left everything to follow Jesus. Yet among the disciples was Peter, the greathearted bumbler; Andrew, the quiet younger brother; James and John, the hotheaded "Sons of Thunder" (Mark 3:17); Matthew, the despised tax collector; Simon, the fire-breathing patriot; Philip, the questioning skeptic; Thomas, the doubter; and Judas Iscariot, the miserly treasurer.

One disciple betrayed Jesus, another denied Him, and all abandoned Him in the hour of His greatest trial. If people are looking for clear evidence of God's power in the New Testament, all they have to do is to see what God was able to do with these unpromising men.

Things did not get much better after Pentecost. The winds of the Spirit and the tongues of fire had barely died down before "the Grecian Jews . . . complained against the Hebraic Jews because their widows were being overlooked in the daily distribution of food" (Acts 6:1). Though there were no fewer than 16 nations represented on the Day of Pentecost (2:8-11), they soon lined up into two major parties divided along ancient racial lines.

Later, Paul's preaching of a gospel of grace that freed them from keeping the minor details of Jewish law precipitated such a crisis that the first ecumenical council of the Church had to be called (15:1-29). One wonders what would have happened to Christianity if the council had voted against accepting Gentile believers unless they embraced the totality of Mosaic Law and rituals.

Shortly after the Jerusalem Council, Paul had such a sharp disagreement with Barnabas over whether to take John Mark—the Church's first "missionary dropout"—with them on their second missionary journey, that they each went their separate ways (vv. 36-41). Later, Paul had a tense confrontation with Peter in front of believers at Antioch over his hypocrisy in withdrawing from and refusing to eat with Gentile Christians, because of how it looked to certain Jewish brethren (Galatians 2:11-14). Even a cursory reading of Paul's letters show the Early Church was quite a diverse crowd.

United Diversity

Any assumption that Christians agree on all points is at best naive and at worst divisive. However, there are areas upon which we must agree. There is a universal aspect to Christianity that finds specific expression within our varied cultures. As the apostle Paul wrote, "There is one body and one Spirit—just as you were called to one hope when you were called—one Lord, one faith, one baptism; one God and Father of all, who is over all and through all and in all" (Ephesians 4:4-6).

Should this not require one united agenda and expression? Yes and no. It gives us unity in the essentials of the faith. There are certain beliefs that must be embraced by all who call themselves Christians. However, the divergence of the faith becomes apparent in our attempts to live these essentials out in our lives. We must all have the same foundation Paul described in verses 4-6. However, he continued, "But to each one of us grace has been given as Christ apportioned it" (v. 7). Here is revealed one of the great paradoxes of the Christian faith—unity through diversity. God's kingdom is composed of inhabitants expressing unique, individual identities, yet committed to a portion of the greater whole, resulting in unity. Thus, while we must embrace the foundational tenets of the faith, we are given freedom to express this faith in differing ways.

This allowance for diversity in expression is God's desire, as He did not create a world of clones. His creation has diversity; so does His kingdom. This has been evident since the beginning.

We have to face the fact that none of us see everything alike. Shortly after our oldest son and his wife were married, we took them on a scenic overnight trip. We stopped along the road so Dean could take a picture of a large herd of elk. Cheryl asked him to give her the camera so she could snap a picture of him over by the fence with the elk in the background.

"I can't get this camera to focus," she complained.

"Just put it on infinity and shoot," he replied.

"It was still out of focus," she said, as she got back in the car. "There must be something wrong with the camera."

A few moments later, I heard her whisper to herself, "Oh, I forgot. I don't have my contacts in."

Each of us reads the Scriptures, thinks about God, and looks at everything through a unique set of lenses. What is truly amazing about the Church is that such a disparate collection of people—coming from so many varied backgrounds and bringing to the table such widely diverse ideas and opinions—are able find any unity at all. Yet the church at Corinth —divisive, immoral, and immature—had so much vitality that Paul could speak of the believers as "sanctified in Christ Jesus and called to be holy" (1 Corinthians 1:2). In spite of their many problems, they had still "been enriched in every way . . . not lack[ing] any spiritual gift" (vv. 5, 7). It is ironic that the Early Church, ruptured by numerous heresies within and rocked by intense persecution from without, exhibited such dynamic spiritual vitality and grew so rapidly that in less than three centuries it conquered Rome without drawing a sword.

One Person's Quest

Few have come to maturity with more twisted misconceptions of God and the Church than Kathleen Norris. She fled Lemmon, South Dakota, when she was 18, in an attempt to escape the cultural and religious environment in which she had been raised. After nearly 20 years wandering in the atheistic and hedonistic wilderness of New York's literary society, she moved back home in search of her geographical and spiritual roots.

In her best-selling books, *Dakota: A Spiritual Geography* and *Amazing Grace,* she tells the story of her long reentry into Christianity.

It was a bitterly cold and windy January morning when she joined the town's small church where her maternal grandmother had been a stalwart member and a beloved Bible teacher for 60 years. When Kathleen heard an elder, whom she never liked much, mumble the words, "I'd like to welcome you to the Body of Christ," she felt a chill. Suddenly, the world seemed larger and opened up in a new way.[1]

Still, she was put off by the infighting and smallness of spirit of so many. Over time, however, Kathleen began to see that the Christian church has always experienced fractiousness and heresy and yet has remained very much alive. Slowly she came to realize that what appeared on the surface to be petulance and immaturity on the part of many were actually desperate cries for help and understanding. One of her pastors reminded her that we go to church for other people, because someone may need us there. She began to see that no matter how wretched she might feel on a given Sunday, it might do someone else good just to see her face or share a conversation over coffee. Someone might be going through a difficult time, and perhaps her word of encouragement would be just enough to carry him or her through.

It was only after she stopped judging the church on how well it ministered to *her*, and began to look for opportunities for ministry to *others*, that the church really came alive for her.[2] She began looking forward to going to church because of the opportunities it offered to touch people's lives. She has since become not only a lay preacher in her grandmother's church but is in demand as a speaker all over the country. Our university's chaplain contacted her and invited her to come to our campus, but found out she is booked up for the next five years!

This is precisely what Jesus was trying to show us when He told His disciples, "Whoever wants to become great among you must be your servant, and whoever wants to be first must be slave of all. For even the Son of Man did not come to be served, but to serve, and to give his life as a ransom for many" (Mark 10:43-45). Few have enunciated this "love ethic"—the only enduring foundation for unity in the midst of diversity—more eloquently than John Wesley:

It is well that you should be thoroughly sensible of this: The heaven of heavens is love. There is nothing higher in religion: there is, in effect, nothing else; if you look for anything more than love, you are looking wide of the mark, you are getting out of the royal way, and when you are asking others, "Have you received this or that blessing?" if you mean anything but more love, you mean wrong; you are leading them out of the way, and putting them upon a false scent. Settle it then in your heart, that from the moment God has saved you from all sin, you are to aim at nothing more, but more of that love described in the thirteenth of Corinthians. You can go no higher till you are carried into Abraham's bosom.[3]

And Finally . . .

Perhaps we're still prone to say, "All Christians are alike." If by this we mean they are forgiven of sin and declared righteous before God, if we mean they are indwelt by the Holy Spirit and are heirs to the Kingdom and coheirs with Christ, if we mean they have the hope of eternity and a peace that passes all understanding, then the statement is correct.

However, if we extend this generality to exclude the uniqueness of God's creation, people, and their expressions in this world, the saying is wrong. We have distorted the faith. Not all Christians are alike. This fact can cause friction among us, but it can also expose us to the rich diversity that encourages and equips the people of God.

Notes:
1. Kathleen Norris, *Amazing Grace* (New York: Penguin Putnam, 1998), 141-42.

2. Ibid., 202-4.

3. John Wesley, *A Plain Account of Christian Perfection* (Albany, Oreg.: AGES Software, 1997), 68-69.

About the Author(s): Dr. Cowles is a religion professor at Point Loma Nazarene University in San Diego. Rev. Mark A. Holmes, senior pastor of Darrow Road Wesleyan Church in Superior, Wisconsin, also contributed to this chapter.

Common Misconception No. 8

Heard Outside the Church: "Christianity is a religion for weak people."
Heard Inside the Church: "Good Christians are meek and turn the other cheek."

Background Scripture: Matthew 5:5; 18:3; 20:26; Luke 22:27; John 19:10-11; 1 Corinthians 1:26-27; 2 Corinthians 12:7-9; Galatians 5:22-23; Ephesians 1:18-20; Philippians 2:6-8

CHAPTER 8

Christians Are Wimps

by Jesse C. Middendorf

"Pastor," he said with a glare, "don't bother me with that stuff. I don't need 'the religion crutch'!" With that, he turned on his heel and walked away.

The media mogul stood with a haughty smirk before the cameras. "I don't need anybody else's god. I am my own god."

"Religion? Christianity? Who needs it?" asked a high school junior.

"Religion is the opiate of the people," said Karl Marx.

"Organized religion is a sham and a crutch for weak-minded people who need strength in numbers," said a former-pro-wrestler-turned-governor.

It wouldn't be so bad if those comments were isolated exceptions to the conversations in the culture at large. But the increasing secularity of the North American culture makes statements like these more the norm than many Christians are willing to acknowledge.

The culture listens to the terms Christians learned from Jesus, and the caricature is reinforced. Jesus said: "The meek . . . will inherit the earth" (Matthew 5:5). "Whoever wants to become great among you must be your servant" (20:26). "Unless you . . . become like little children, you will never enter the kingdom of heaven" (18:3). "I am among you as one who serves" (Luke 22:27).

Even in our leadership training, they hear it. We refer to "servant leadership." One of our controlling metaphors is the basin and towel, symbolic of the example of Jesus, who stooped before His disciples and washed their feet.

Where does it lead us? After all, didn't Jesus say that when we are struck, we are to turn the other cheek; that we are not to resist the one who seeks to borrow from us; and that if compelled to carry the weapons of a soldier one mile, we should voluntarily carry them a second mile?

If Christianity is ever to win the world, how can it do so with one hand tied behind its back?

"I am the master of my fate; / I am the captain of my soul," wrote the poet William Ernest Henley. And the popular culture shouts a loud and resounding "Yes!" It says, "We don't need the crutch of religion, the demeaning and obsequious humility that demands that we hang our heads in shame for our humanity. Let's hear it for the human potential movement!" They go on to urge, "Let's reject the meek and mild Jesus in favor of a more robust and rigorous figure, one who can challenge our deeper self, who calls us to an appreciation of our innate capabilities, our unique strengths, and our indomitable spirit."

Maybe Christians feel better when the image is that of the grace and coordination of a gifted and handsome athlete who, scoring the winning touchdown, holds his hand high, finger pointed toward the skies, and shouts with religious zeal, "Thank You, Jesus!" No weakness there. "We beat the other guys because Jesus heard our prayer!" "God loves a winner!" "Don't give in to weakness! Be strong in the Lord!" "Power—that's the picture!"

Or do we prefer the image of the hardworking entrepreneur who, sacrificing time and energies to build a successful company, testifies that God honors the daring and the strong? "God helps those who help themselves!" "Lead, follow, or get out of the way!" "Strength—that is the key!"

In a world intoxicated with power and enamored with strength, what hope is there for the Christian message? How does that message "compete" in the marketplace of beliefs and ideas when the images and metaphors of Christianity seem so out of touch?

The Corinthian Context

The church in first-century Corinth was a curious mixture. While we do not know the exact sociological and demographic makeup of the believers there, we do have hints that the congregation was made up of the lowly and the noble, the powerful and the weak (1 Corinthians 1:26). Slaves and masters worshiped together, and the uneasy congregation found itself struggling with how the story of a crucified and risen Messiah could provide a basis for peaceful coexistence in the face of such wide diversity.

Into the midst of ideas and perspectives that were a part of that conflicted church, Paul dropped a stunning revelation of the majesty of God's grace: "Not many of you were wise by human standards; not many were influential; not many were of noble birth. But God chose the foolish things of the world to shame the wise; God chose the weak things of the world to shame the strong" (vv. 26-27).

Whatever the human measures of value and significance, says Paul, God has disgraced them by overturning their warped perspectives.

The Christian Context

Whenever we deal with issues of strength and weakness in the context of the Christian life, it is easy to allow our concepts to be defined by a secular worldview, which either fails or refuses to take note of the nature of strength as defined in a Christian worldview.

Throughout Scripture, however, we encounter a different understanding of power. The expectations of the natural order—that might makes right, that the physically strong always prevail, that weakness and vulnerability are suspect and without value—are upended.

While on one level the story of David and Goliath is a delightful children's story that we love to tell, at another level we easily dismiss the significance of such stories for an adult world where real opponents are closer and more threatening. We are less willing to embrace the belief that our weakness is an opportunity for God to work. We want to be sure we are armed to the hilt in case we find ourselves in a fight where the odds are stacked against us.

But what did Jesus mean when He said, "Blessed are the meek"? Was He putting a premium on human frailty? Was He really expecting us to live in a threatening world with our weapons of defense surrendered and our vulnerabilities exaggerated?

The Nature of Our Strength

Though we use words like "power" and "strength" as if there were a common understanding of their meaning, Scripture reveals a profoundly different kind of strength is at work in the life of the believer.

At one level, we acknowledge that physical strength and mental prowess are natural abilities. Being human is itself a gift of God, and every person is capable of exercising natural capabilities that are amazing when examined carefully and objectively. This is the result of God's good creation. Though there are glaring and heartbreaking exceptions due to defect and disease, the vast majority of humanity is capable of amazing feats of strength and intelligence, especially when compared to other creatures and forms of life.

And when mere force of will or physical prowess or mental ability is at issue, it appears that the strong do prevail, the intelligent do dominate, the willful exercise dominion.

But Scripture dares to suggest that there is a domain, to which all creation must ultimately submit, in which strength is of a different kind. It is spiritual. It has its source in God. It is not separate and distinct from the physical realm, but it is the undergirding reality that gives meaning and substance to the tangible, the real.

As Jesus stood before Pilate in the judgment hall, Pilate struggled to understand this silently strong prisoner who was the object of such hatred from the Jews. Unsure of how to interpret the charges by the religious leaders and troubled by the calm, silent demeanor of his prisoner, Pilate challenged Jesus, "Don't you realize I have power either to free you or to crucify you?" (John 19:10).

The response of Jesus froze Pilate in his tracks. "You would have no power over me if it were not given to you from above" (v. 11). In that moment, Jesus relativized every form of earthly, human power. It finds its meaning in relation to its Source, or it is corrupt and ultimately defeated.

The Measure of Our Power

"Knowledge is power," say the historians and educators of the world. By human measure, history has proved the validity of this assertion. The pen is indeed mightier than the sword. The amazing feats of human achievement and progress made possible by scientific inquiry are self-evident. And the capability of communicating knowledge to the masses through the myriad of technologies available to us makes the dissemination of knowledge to the farthest reaches of the globe possible.

Recent history has indicated that once access to knowledge is given to people, revolutions occur. And yes, all too frequently, "Might makes right." Military power and political systems suppress peoples, forcing them into subservience and wreaking havoc as villages and towns are reduced to rubble by rockets and bombs.

We measure the explosive power of bombs in megatons and the thrust of rockets in tens of thousands of pounds. We see strength demonstrated in the building of huge skyscrapers in our cities worldwide. Yet, all the human and scientific measures of power prove to be woefully inadequate in the face of disease, natural disaster, and death.

The apostle Paul, writing to the church in Ephesus, spoke of a measure of power that is beyond every human capability and measure. He prayed that the Ephesian Christians might "know the hope" to which they were called in Christ, might know "the riches of his glorious inheritance in the saints," and that they might know "his incomparably great power for us who believe" (1:18-19).

In a stunning assertion, Paul declared that the power he desired them to know, to experience, is "like the working of his mighty strength, which he exerted in Christ when he raised him from the dead" (vv. 19-20). Often Christians fail to grasp the profound implications of that prayer. Paul was simply saying to us that the power that raised Jesus from the dead is the power that is at work in the life of the believer!

Scientific advances over the last century have been staggering. Measures of power and strength have exceeded human imagination. The harnessing of the atom, the development of technologies for space exploration, and advances in medical science have far exceeded human expectations. Nevertheless, given all the advances in technology, knowledge, power, and human capability, we have yet to develop a power equal to that which God exerted in order to raise Jesus from the dead.

The greatest difficulty for many believers is in understanding and utilizing *that* power. Hemmed in by the secular definitions and human measures of might, the Christian may be tempted to view power in finite categories. Still, Jesus was unmistakable in His rejection of human conceptions of power. Repeatedly, He insisted that His followers embrace a servant attitude, that they become as little children, that they follow His example as their Master.

In his letter to the Christians in Philippi, Paul described the attitude of Jesus: "Who, being in very nature God, did not consider equality with God something to be grasped, but made himself nothing, taking the very nature of a servant, being made in human likeness. . . . He humbled himself and became obedient to death" (2:6-8).

In a self-sufficient culture, those are hard words to read. In a world that values self-assertion and self-promotion, the example of Jesus seems inadequate and beneath our dignity. Still, the very expression of His humiliation became the greatest measure of the strength of Jesus. Throughout the centuries, His followers have found that example to be a source of profound and effective strength for them. His call to servanthood and self-surrender rings true and provides the believer with a graphic illustration of the proper uses of power.

When Jesus taught His followers to turn the other cheek, it was not because it was easy or would bring quick appreciation and response. Jesus understood the power of a soft answer. He also understood that a soft answer was no guarantee of a kind reaction from others. At the cost of His own life, He demonstrated the vulnerability of a righteous cause pursued with single-minded intensity but rejection of the typical exercises of power. And He taught His followers to lay down their lives, if necessary, for each other.

The Objective of Our Power

The apostle Paul was very candid in his admission of frailty and vulnerability. Writing to the Corinthians, he recounted his own struggle with a "thorn in [the] flesh, a messenger of Satan, to torment" him (2 Corinthians 12:7). Three times he pleaded with the Lord to deliver him from the tormenting condition or circumstance (see v. 8). The response to his pleas has provided a source of encouragement for believers for two millennia.

The Lord said to Paul, "My grace is sufficient for you, for my power is made perfect in weakness."

"Therefore," said Paul, "I will boast all the more gladly about my weaknesses, *so that Christ's power may rest on me*" (v. 9, emphasis added).

The true measure of the power of the believer is not our human strength, wisdom, or physical prowess. It is the power of Christ. And the purpose of that power is to reveal Christ. It is the objective of God that, through the power of the Holy Spirit, the power of the risen Christ, our lives might be the avenue through which others are ushered into relation with Him.

The purpose of God's power in us is not the mere demonstration of personal purity. His purifying presence is a reality we may desire, and for which we may legitimately seek. But it is not the only end toward which He intends us to experience His power. Rather, He desires that the power that is at work in us be exercised in redemptive endeavors, in compassionate ministries, in relationships that reflect the priorities and values that defined Jesus while He ministered with His followers on the earth.

The power of the believer is demonstrated in the "fruit of the Spirit . . . love, joy, peace, patience, kindness, goodness, faithfulness, gentleness and self-control" (Galatians 5:22-23). Those are descriptions of relationship. They are the means by which we exercise the power of the Holy Spirit in the give-and-take of the home, the job, the neighborhood, and the church. They are not window dressing, mere dimensions of a pleasing personality, or the outcome only of careful discipline. They are the demonstration of the Spirit. They do not come full-grown and mature but must be cultivated and nurtured to maturity, often under pressure and in difficult circumstances. They are demonstrations of power in the life of a believer, not natural abilities. Some may find them more easily brought to maturity than others, because of natural affinity; but even so, they require the power of God to find fullest and most effective expression.

And the purpose is that our relationships may be redemptive.

Are Christians Wimps?

Try living the fruit of the Spirit on your own. Try living the Sermon on the Mount in the daily give-and-take of life. Try facing the harsh criticisms of the secular culture directed toward those who would dare to live their faith in the marketplace or the statehouse.

And try bringing someone to faith in Christ in your own strength and wisdom. It will tend to sound like foolishness and the loud clash of irritating cymbals.

However, empowered by the Spirit, the "foolishness" of the message takes on the dynamic of the Resurrection, and people you had not dreamed could change become living demonstrations of mercy and grace.

Wimps? Hardly! Weak? Decidedly! But possessed of a

power that makes the least and the unable into the unstoppable instruments of God.

About the Author: Dr. Middendorf serves as general superintendent in the Church of the Nazarene.

Common Misconception No. 9

Heard Outside the Church: "The
  Church is full of hypocrites."
Heard Inside the Church: "There are no
  hypocrites in our church."

Background Scripture: Matthew 5:48; 6;
  7:3-5, 14; 12:35-37; 23:13, 15, 23, 25,
  27, 29; John 8:32; 17:17; Romans 2:15;
  7:21-23; 1 Corinthians 7:5; Philippians 2:12

CHAPTER 9

Hypocrisy: The Mother of All Vices

by Gerard Reed

A century ago Mark Twain chatted with a ruthless business-man, one of the famed robber barons who ruled like feudal lords over the Gilded Age. The businessman was widely not-ed for his weekly presence in his church, for donating rather publicly to many Christian endeavors. He was equally renowned, however, for his "might makes right" business tac-tics, for devouring competitors by any means necessary as he accumulated his fortune.

In the conversation with Twain, he ventured to impress the writer by piously proclaiming, "Before I die, I mean to make a pilgrimage to the Holy Land. I will climb Mount Sinai and read the Ten Commandments aloud at the top."

Twain replied, "I have a better idea. You could stay home in Boston and keep them."[1]

Straight Talk

Agreeing with another ancient quip, Twain no doubt saw that the robber baron illustrated the truth that "hypocrisy is the homage that vice pays to virtue." Yet, with Twain, most of us decry hypocrisy. From others, especially, we want straight talk: "Say what you mean! Mean what you say!" "Walk your talk!" "Stop pretending to be what you're not!" "Avoid hypocrisy!"

Fifty years ago, a straight-talking Texas congressman, Maury Maverick, coined the word "gobbledygook," effective-ly labeling the kind of mystifying language routinely evident in those bureaucratic memos and political manifestos that seem designed to perplex. He explained that he was probably "thinking of the old bearded turkey gobbler back in Texas who was always gobbley gobbling and strutting with ludicrous pomposity. At the end of its gobble, there was a sort of gook." Against such pretense, against all perversions of our language, Maverick protested, saying: "A man's language is a very important part of his conduct. He should be held morally responsible for his words, just as he is accountable for his other acts."[2]

Most of us, with the congressman, share Homer's ancient view voiced in the *Iliad:* "I detest that man who hides one thing in the depths of his heart and speaks forth another." Equally adamant, Jesus said: "The good man brings good things out of the good stored up in him, and the evil man brings evil things out of the evil stored up in him. But I tell you that men will have to give account on the day of judgment for every careless word they have spoken. For by your words you will be acquitted, and by your words you will be condemned" (Matthew 12:35-37).

Secular thinkers, such as Congressman Maverick, remind us that hypocrisy is not a vice unique to Christianity! Truth to tell, hypocrisy laces all human history with its subtle, distorting, "invisible ink" qualities. It haunts the classrooms of prestigious university professors as well as the studios of televangelists. It subverts health-care facilities as easily as ecclesiastical institutions. Ever since Adam and Eve tried to evade the truth and hide the evidence concerning their disobedience in Eden, their descendants have engaged in devious, misleading speech and behavior.

Consequently, Jesus rebuked the hypocrisy of the scribes and Pharisees—the religious leaders in first-century Palestine. The sharpness of His indictment, the stinging clarity of His words, show how deeply He detested phony speech and devious acts. In Matthew 6, He charged His followers to avoid the hypocrisy of "showboat" praying, fasting, and giving alms. In Matthew 23, the chapter in that Gospel that records the bulk of Jesus' critique of hypocrisy, He repeated six times, "Woe to you, teachers of the law and Pharisees, you hypocrites!" (vv. 13, 15, 23, 25, 27, 29). He condemned the practice, too common in His day, of religious doublespeak, of talking one way and acting in another. To seek the most prominent places in synagogue events while mistreating widows and orphans, to make a show of tithing minor items while treating others unjustly, leaves one outwardly righteous but inwardly rotten.

The Mother of All Vices

The seriousness of the issue is clarified by James S. Spiegel. Hypocrisy, he asserts, is "the mother of all vices."[3] Like a blood clot entering the aorta, hypocrisy lies right at the heart of moral failure. Spiegel underscores what a Jewish philosopher, Hannah Arendt, asserted when she declared that "it is plausible to assume that hypocrisy is the vice of vices" and that "the hypocrite is really rotten to the core" because he or she deliberately denies the truth of his or her inner essence.[4]

The word "hypocrisy" comes from the Greek *hypocrisis*, which means playing a role on stage. Performing on TV or strutting about on a theater stage have little to do with living a real life. So "hypocrisy" means playing a role, mouthing the words of a script that have little to do with a real self. The classic Greek tragedian Euripides saw it well in 420 B.C. He wrote in the play *Electra*, "Often a noble face hides filthy ways." Plato, also, penciling in some of the marks of an unjust person in *The Republic* in 360 B.C., noted that he or she "must act as clever [ones] do" by seeming to be "just without being so."

Thomas Aquinas, blending Greek definitions into Christian theology around A.D. 1265, condemned hypocrisy as a kind of "dissimulation," whereby one deliberately lies through deceptive deeds. Such "dissimulation" is deadly, because it subtly subverts the "truth itself," the fundamental integrity needed for righteousness. Hypocrisy, Aquinas says, is a devious and serpentine vice because it tries to blend sin and sanctity—the lack of holiness and the appearance of holiness—so as to sculpt the bust of an upright person out of rotten material.

Not Everything Is Hypocrisy

Rightly defined, then, hypocrisy must never be confused with irritating inconsistencies that may seem, at first sight, to illustrate it. With so serious a vice to consider, we must weigh our words as carefully as an assayer weighs gold and silver. We can, using Scripture and reason, string barbed wire fences around the vice of hypocrisy. Importantly, there is a clearly discernible difference between the Greek words *hypocrisis* and *akrasia*. The former indicates a deliberate deviousness, a malicious intent, while the latter points out a moral weakness, a lack of self-disciplining strength, which cannot always be avoided. We may very well promise more than we can deliver, as when we assure someone we will "always be there" for them, but such is not hypocrisy. We may easily profess, in a moment of confidence, more than we can actually perform, but such is not hypocrisy. The Greek word *akrasia*, translated (in 1 Corinthians 7:5) as the lack of "self-control," indicates that we often fail, not because we are phony, but because we lack the strength of character to live as we know we ought.

Sins of weakness—*akrasia*—result from caving in to one's physical hungers, one's nonrational desires. It's like slipping, as if on a bobsled run, into a behavior one rationally disapproves but cannot at the moment control. Some physical desires—as we know when we take "just one more piece of chocolate candy"—simply overwhelm our reasonable, "better" self. The best of our good intentions, the highest of our New Year's resolutions, get easily derailed when we're overwhelmed with longings for special pleasures. So Aristotle (384-322 B.C.) in his *Ethics* called "incontinent" the person afflicted with *akrasia* who cannot control himself or herself, who knowingly does wrong, yet "does it as a result of passion, while the continent [the self-controlled one], knowing that his [or her] appetites are bad, refuses on account of . . . rational principle to follow them."

This, it seems clear, is also the Bible's position, which is confirmed by human experience. We often encounter people who act counter to their best judgment and illustrate the corrosive power of sin lodged deeply in their souls. Still, we're encouraged (and actually deeply desire as Christians) to exert self-control over our desires so as to live a godly life.

Paul's probing discussion in Romans 7 perfectly portrays this natural inner tension: "When I want to do good, evil is right there with me. For in my inner being I delight in God's law; but I see another law at work in the members of my body, waging war against the law of my mind and making me a prisoner of the law of sin at work within my members" (vv. 21-23).

This is what we often call "original sin"—the "bent toward evil" characteristic that plagues our species and that calls for the purifying work of the Holy Spirit. Yet, most of our actual sins—the sins we personally, deliberately commit—demonstrate *akrasia*, not *hypocrisis*.

Overcoming Hypocrisy

So, when Christians are accused of "hypocrisy," as we often are, we must resolutely filter out spurious charges before responding. There's a big difference between sin and hypocrisy. The church, of course, is a place where sinners can find salvation. So Christians welcome sinners to join them in attending church, to repent and seek forgiveness, to struggle with their sins without being rejected for their failures. Furthermore, it is often difficult to live as Christians ideally should live. It's easier to wear a "What Would Jesus Do?" bracelet than to follow His example on a daily basis. So we who follow Jesus fly the highest of all ideals—to be "perfect" as God is perfect (Matthew 5:48). Yet, coming down to earth, we frequently fall short in many ways.

Ironically, folks who accuse Christians of hypocrisy get their very idea of moral perfection from Christian teaching. If the standards weren't so high, it would be harder to fault the faithful for failing to measure up. Were we seeking to follow a less-than-perfect Lord—perhaps a charismatic leader like Peter, with highly visible flaws—we'd have less trouble succeeding. But sin, multifaceted and alluring, keeps us from perfectly following a sinless Christ. Satan, cunning and shrewd, misleads us. So to sin and confess our sins—even glaring, outrageous sins—does not, in any way, embroil us in the muck of "hypocrisy."

Nevertheless, having insisted that *akrasia* differs from *hypocrisis*, we must also admit that hypocrisy has forever plagued the Christian community. In part, this results from a perversion of one of the Church's great truths—that we're saved by grace alone. Given the incredible goodness of this gospel message, it's easy for some folks to play the Christian "game"—to talk the talk without walking the walk. They easily take refuge in God's "amazing grace," which in their case is mainly amazing in its ability to mask their waywardness. So there will always be some truth to the charge that the Church is "filled with hypocrites." The very strength of the gospel—grace—can easily be twisted into an excuse for duplicity.

Still more, when Christians take too seriously the call to "work out your salvation with fear and trembling" (Philippians 2:12), we easily forget the humbling emotions, "fear and trembling," and slip into a hypercritical spirit, condemning folks who seem less committed, less righteous, less "good" than ourselves. Jesus addressed this issue in Matthew 7:3-5, where He insisted that we remove the plank from our own eye before we try to remove a splinter from our neighbor's.

We must, of course, judge certain behaviors wrong. We can denounce sin without condemning sinners. Jesus routinely did so, as is evident in His denunciation of hypocrisy. To witness a robbery should lead us to report the crooks. To see racism riddling a community should prod us to protest. To learn that a city council member has been stealing from the tax revenues should elicit a strong "judgment" against such malfeasance. To see how pornography perverts our society should lead us to condemn and curtail its purveyors.

But we're instructed to leave the judging of others' spiritual condition, their eternal estate, to God. When we take a holier-than-thou stance, when we continually point out others' spiritual shortcomings so as to highlight our own superiority, we slip into a judgmentalism that fully deserves the label hypocrisy.

Living Without Hypocrisy

Rightly defined, hypocrisy clearly results from our difficulty in yoking together what we *think* with what we *say* and what we *do*. We need to think truthfully, speak honestly, and live virtuously. Many hypocrites fail to think truthfully, to deal honestly with God's law, to recognize His rules. They are, basically, "amoralists," folks who claim there are no moral norms, freeing themselves from any responsibilities. The very worst form of hypocrisy is to pretend that no moral standards exist, for it is a denial of what Paul declared is "written on their hearts" (Romans 2:15).

Still more, hypocrites generally—and generously—indulge in self-deception. They manage to concoct elaborate defense mechanisms, which enable them to avoid dealing with the truth. Self-deception is preferring to live with illusions, daydreams, and imagined utopias. If there's a tumor growing in someone's stomach, he or she can, of course, ignore the doctor's diagnosis and pretend there is no cancer, even while it devours the innards. And we can pretend we're right with God, ignoring all that's said in Scripture and tradition, while sin atrophies our souls.

In view of all this, how can we live hypocrisy-free? The antidote to the poison of hypocrisy is truth. Jesus said to His followers, "You will know the truth, and the truth will set you free" (John 8:32). We are, He said, to be sanctified "by the truth" (17:17). To abolish hypocrisy, we must allow the light of truth to shine on our inner selves. With great clarity, Miguel Cervantes urged, "Make it thy business to know thyself, which is the most difficult lesson in the world." And Fyodor Dostoyevsky said much the same in *The Brothers Karama-*

zov: "Above all, don't lie to yourself. The man who lies to himself and listens to his own lie comes to such a pass that he cannot distinguish the truth within him, or around him, and so loses all respect for himself and for others. And having no respect he ceases to love, and in order to occupy and distract himself without love he gives way to passions and coarse pleasures, and sinks to bestiality in his vices, all from continual lying to other men and to himself."[5]

We've always known, of course, that the virtuous path, the way of holiness, is a demanding, "narrow" way (Matthew 7:14). Still, it's eternally worth the effort. It's a lesson we often seek to circumvent, taking recourse in dishonest games and phony facades. Yet, if we can see and accept the truth about ourselves, it is possible to live that truth.

Notes:

1. Clifton Fadiman, ed., *The Little Brown Book of Anecdotes* (Boston: Little Brown and Co., 1985), 554.

2. William Lambdin, ed., *The Doublespeak Dictionary* (Los Angeles: Pinnacle Books, 1979), 98.

3. James S. Spiegel, *Hypocrisy: Moral Fraud and Other Vices* (Grand Rapids: Baker Books, 1999), 113.

4. Hannah Arendt, *On Revolution* (New York: Viking Press, 1963), 99.

5. Fyodor Dostoyevsky, *The Brothers Karamazov,* trans. Constance Garnett (New York: William Heinemann, 1945), 37-38.

About the Author: Dr. Reed is university chaplain as well as professor of history, philosophy, and religion at Point Loma Nazarene University, San Diego.

Common Misconception No. 10

Heard Outside the Church: "The Christian idea of fun is a Bible study."
Heard Inside the Church: "Christianity is serious business."

Background Scripture: Genesis 17:17; 21:16; Job 41:1-34; Psalm 126:1-2; Matthew 6:16; John 15:10-11; 2 Corinthians 5:17; Philippians 4:4; 2 Timothy 2:3; James 1:2-3; 1 Peter 1:8; 4:12; Jude 24

CHAPTER 10

Faith and Fun: Not at All like Oil and Water

by Jon Johnston

Some time ago I spoke to a Saudi Arabian university student about his Muslim faith. Specifically, I asked him when he planned to make his "hajj," a required, once-in-a-lifetime pilgrimage to Mecca. With a sheepish grin he replied, "Not until I'm a very old man."

Curious, I asked, "Is there a particular reason?"

He responded, "Oh, yes. In Islam, after going on the holy pilgrimage, you're supposed to really shape up—and stay that way for the rest of your life. No more wild parties and carousing, as I'm enjoying now. So I'm postponing the trip until I'm practically on my deathbed."

For this fellow, getting serious about his faith meant one thing: squelching most everything he associated with enjoying life. Being holy and happy, in his mind, were totally incompatible. This same attitude is prevalent throughout our culture today.

A Portrait That Doesn't Do Us Justice

The media delights in portraying Christianity as straitlaced, restrictive, somber (even morbid), and formalistic. Indeed, something best suited for stuffy, self-righteous bores.

Why? To the secular world, fun is strictly associated with sensuality. That means letting out all the stops. No moral restraints, even if it means acting irresponsibly or wacky. Believers who have strong faith and convictions are perceived as killjoys. Old before their time. Little more than a conglomeration of inhibitions. Uptight people who never unpack the suitcases from their never-ending guilt trips.

It would be bad enough if only outsiders to the faith believed this inaccurate viewpoint, but it isn't confined to them. To a significant degree, it has taken root among Christians, and the effects are devastating.

Stained-glass Sullenness

In the proud tradition of the Pharisees, many church folks equate seriousness with respect for God. They feel that it provides an impression of not traveling the world's road of hilarity, superficiality, and sensuality. Fun, accordingly, is seen as the devil's "bait"—the springboard to sin. Since sin is such a gravely serious matter, their somber countenances properly reflect their attitudes toward it.

John Wesley, though a man who was jovial upon occasion, advised preachers to adopt a serious, weighty, and solemn deportment. Furthermore, he instructed Methodists to "avoid all lightness, jesting and foolish talking."[1] He would have been aghast at some very humorous comments I've heard at Christian gatherings!

But what about the present? Do folks equate holy living with sedate and somber demeanor? Absolutely, which prompts kids to confront their parents with the question: "Do we have to go to church today, or can we go have fun?" It still causes outsiders to wince at the mere mention of religion. Why? They assume it throws a wet blanket over any hopes of living an enjoyable life. Thus, they agree with the Saudi student: it's to be avoided or postponed until the last moments of life.

What about this perception? Should Christian faith and fun be considered totally incompatible? Conversely, does a life of sin have a monopoly on true enjoyment? Let's examine some facts that many Christians ignore and most secularists contest.

A Reason for Holy Hilarity

God's Word emphatically discloses that the Christian walk should be the opposite of doom and gloom. There are countless references to joy, gladness, rejoicing, and happiness. Where these exist, there is always plenty of laughter. Not surprisingly, the Old Testament speaks of laughter over 50 times.

Though Abraham at first laughed at God's promise to give him a son by his 90-year-old wife (Genesis 17:17), his scoffing was replaced by Sarah's joyful laughter at the birth of Isaac. She said, "God has brought me laughter" (21:6).

When the Israelites came back to their homeland from their foreign exile, the psalmist sang of the occasion. "When the LORD brought back the captives to Zion, we were like men who dreamed. Our mouths were filled with laughter, our tongues with songs of joy" (126:1-2).

Does this same theme continue in the New Testament? The answer should not surprise us.

Jesus declared to His followers: "When you fast, do not look somber as the hypocrites [sanctimonious fakes and exhibitionists] do" (Matthew 6:16). At the Last Supper—knowing that He was soon to be arrested, tried, cursed, beaten, spit upon, and crucified—our Lord proclaimed to His disciples: "If you obey my commands, you will remain in my love. . . . I have told you this so that my joy may be in you and that your joy may be complete" (John 15:10-11).

However, the joy He speaks of far transcends, and sharply contrasts with, the fun that this world pursues. Let's examine a few of the most crucial differences:

Christ's joy:
- ❏ Permanent and ever-increasing satisfaction
- ❏ Primarily spiritual, though includes the senses
- ❏ Springs forth from within
- ❏ Is based on our relationship with Him
- ❏ Never gravitates to debased gutter humor or sadism

World's fun/happiness:
- ❏ Temporary and ever-diminishing satisfaction
- ❏ Exclusively sensual

❑ Prompted from external stimuli

❑ Not grounded on a relationship

❑ Often drifts toward the immoral, cruel, or sacrilegious

A gospel song that is a favorite of many Christians calls our relationship to Jesus "Joy Unspeakable." Why? Because our Lord is the essence of life, light, love—and laughter. In short, He makes all things new (2 Corinthians 5:17) when He gifts us with all four of these. Thereafter, the well from which we draw our enjoyment is of a different kind. Sure, we chuckle at humorous, clean jokes, but we also have a joyful time seeing others happy, hearing of answered prayers, and reminding ourselves that, on the last page of His great Book, His (and our) side triumphs over evil. To put it bluntly, we have the last laugh. So, who has greater reason to joyfully celebrate?

No wonder the apostle Paul declared to the Philippians, "Rejoice in the Lord always. I will say it again: Rejoice!" (4:4). And why, in his letter to dispersed Christians, Peter spoke of being "filled with an inexpressible and glorious joy" because of the gift of salvation (1 Peter 1:8). James, for his part, instructed Christians to consider it "pure joy" when facing trials—for they develop perseverance (1:2-3). And Jude chimes in with: "All glory to God, who is able to keep you from stumbling, and who will bring you into his glorious presence innocent of sin and with great joy" (v. 24, NLT).

Thus, we see that the basic tenor of the Scriptures is joy, which both calms us in suffering and exalts us in flowing blessings. Indeed, in God's Word the appropriate responses to our life in Christ are exuberant thankfulness, excited praise, exultant joy, effervescent smiles, and erupting laughter. Upbeat rather than downcast. Positive rather than pathetic. Rejoicing rather than regretful. Anticipating rather than anguishing.

Some of My Heroes

Most of us have little trouble being positive and winsome when things go well: a job promotion, our child's honor roll achievement, a clean bill of health, or a special blessing by God's Spirit. Still, some folks keep smiling in the midst of life's storms. When they've been pummeled by tragedy, it truly defies this world's logic.

In the face of extreme adversity and persecution, the early Christian martyrs maintained a joyful and gentle spirit. Yet when pondering their lives, we're prone to focus only on their heart-wrenching suffering and overlook the fact that most had an incredible sense of humor. Many even laughed in the face of their tormentors and executioners moments before they were beheaded, thrown to lions, crucified, hanged, or burned to death.

When Roman soldiers arrived to arrest Ignatius of Antioch (A.D. 107), informed that he would be fed to the lions in the Flavian Amphitheater, he declared, "I have joy of the beasts that are prepared for me." Polycarp (A.D. 155) was arrested and told to deny his faith or be burned at the stake. His response: "Bring against me what you please." A witness observed that "whilst he said this, he appeared in a transport of joy and confidence, and his countenance shown with a certain heavenly grace." The fires were lit, and he died.

Agnes (A.D. 304) was courted by numerous Roman noblemen attracted to her beauty and riches, but she consecrated herself to Jesus. During the Diocletian persecution, she was condemned to be beheaded. Ambrose wrote: "Agnes, filled with joy on hearing this sentence, went to the place of execution more cheerfully than others go to their wedding."

Vincent of Saragossa, a contemporary of Agnes, was stretched on the rack, and his flesh was torn with iron hooks. Smiling, he called the executioners fainthearted. His persecutors then rubbed his wounds with salt and put him on a gridiron of red-hot fire with bars full of spikes. Witnesses reported that "Vincent mounted cheerfully the iron bed." Augustine later wrote that Vincent suffered torments far beyond what any man could have endured unless supported by supernatural strength. "The more he suffered, the greater seemed to be the inward joy and consolation of his soul."[2]

Volumes could not do justice to the thousands of Christians—known and unknown—who suffered martyrdom for their faith at the hands of unbelievers or intolerant believers. Many were martyred in Nazi Germany and in Communist Russia. Sadly, more are being persecuted and slain today than ever before. But be assured, as in the past, God is giving them a special joy. Archbishop Oscar Romero of San Salvador, killed by an assassin's bullet in 1980, offered this homily shortly before his death: "It is wrong to be sad. Christians cannot be pessimists. Christians must always nourish in their hearts the fullness of joy. Try it, brothers and sisters; I have tried it many times and in the darkest moments, when slander and persecution were at their worst: to unite myself intimately with Christ, my friend. . . . It is the deepest joy the heart can have."[3]

Nevertheless, how about those of us who aren't martyrs? Some of us are hit hard by unfortunate circumstances and nagging, persistent problems: Demons from the past. People who delight in making our lives miserable. Health difficulties that get progressively worse.

As with the martyrs, God can minister healing and comfort to our aching and throbbing hearts. If it is within His will, He can change things in an eye blink, so we must be persistent in prayer. On the other hand, when things stay the same or get worse, He offers grace to help us get through it—and with a jubilant spirit. Millions through the annals of history can testify to this.

What Joyfulness Yields

To join in with the chorus of biblical authors, martyrs, and ordinary people who advocate living lives that exude irrepressible joy is not to see all bad times suddenly evaporate. Timothy referred to true Christians as soldiers who must endure hardship (2 Timothy 2:3). Peter spoke of suffering as a "painful trial" that is sure to try us (1 Peter 4:12).

Furthermore, we cannot count on perpetually residing on an emotional mountaintop. Our spirits will sometimes sink, due to temperament cycles, crises overload, or Satan's power. Sometimes we don't feel like sporting a big grin and don't especially appreciate others telling us that we should.

Still, having said this, there is great advantage in allowing God to cultivate within us a positive, expectant attitude and cheerful countenance. Focus on the doughnut, not the hole; the half-full rather than half-empty glass. In spite of our dog days and temporary slips, the profile of our lives can increasingly gravitate in this direction—as we deepen our walk with Him and remind ourselves of His blessings.

Conclusion

As we all know, seriousness isn't always to be shunned. When repenting of our sins, expressing condolences to the bereaved, or reflecting on a threatening health issue, we should be somber and reflective.

Conversely, a happy countenance isn't always good. In both Old and New Testaments there is the laughter of the unrighteous, who often mocked or laughed to scorn God and the prophets.

Nevertheless, concerning the laughter and joy of the righteous, God's Word invariably lauds its existence. It is positive, energizing, therapeutic, healthy—even holy. As one wisely stated: "We ought to take humor more seriously!" Why? Because we Christians are the people of hope.

Notes:

1. "Minutes of Several Conversations Between the Rev. Mr. Wesley and Others; From the year 1744, to the year 1789," *Addresses, Essays, Letters,* vol. 8 of *The Complete Works of John Wesley* (Albany, Oreg.: AGES Software, 1997), 359.

2. Cal Samra, *The Joyful Christ: The Healing Power of Humor* (San Francisco: Harper and Row Publishers, 1985), 92-101.

3. Ibid.

About the Author: Dr. Johnston is a professor of sociology at Pepperdine University (Malibu, California) and president of the Association of Nazarene Sociologists of Religion (ANSR).

Common Misconception No. 11

Heard Outside the Church: "Christianity is just an emotional experience."

Heard Inside the Church: "Truly spiritual experiences are always emotional ones."

Background Scripture: Matthew 22:37-39; 26:38, 42; Mark 1:40-41; 3:5; 10:21; Luke 7:13; 10:21; 19:41-44; John 11:3, 35, 38; Galatians 5:22-23

CHAPTER 11

Christianity Is Just an Emotional Experience

by Randy T. Hodges

His outspoken remarks knocked many religiously sensitive people back on their heels. "Organized religion is a sham and a crutch for weak-minded people who need strength in numbers," said Minnesota governor Jesse Ventura.[1]

Maybe you reacted like me. Even if he believed his own words, how could a high-profile, elected official say such a thing?

Ventura's willingness to speak his mind left no doubt where he stands on religion. Yet, like it or not, the remark points to a view of life that is held by more and more people around us. Many of those outside the church are disillusioned by—and even hostile to—organized religion. Many conclude that there is really nothing to religion. At best, they believe that Christianity is just an emotional experience.

When we begin to consider how to fit authentic religion and emotions together, we find that even those in the church struggle to know how to unite them.

Jim Spruce recalls one of God's saints from his early experience in the church:

I remember him only because he shared the quietly eloquent language of tears. At times his great shoulders heaved under the weight of burden. Yet there was never a hint of attention getting, of hoarse bawling. You'd find his form always lovely, never self-seeking. When I asked about him, Dad remarked, "He is a true Jeremiah, a weeping prophet of our day." For all I know, he wept for me, too.

Few were just like him. But I remember others who walked the aisles and shouted and praised God, who waved handkerchiefs, who lifted their hands heavenward, who laughed the innocent laugh of holy joy. I never doubted their authenticity in demonstration.[2]

Remembering days when emotional expression was more common in public worship, some struggle with the haunting thought that the church today can't possibly be as godly as it once was, since it certainly is less emotional. At the core of their struggle is the idea that only emotional experiences are spiritual. Because getting a handle on genuine spirituality is tough, some equate emotion with spirituality.

The conclusions of those outside the church, as well as those within it, lead to a common concern: What is the proper role of emotions in authentic spirituality? Or, to put it another way, what role does God want our emotions to play in our walk with Him?

Wrestling with this question by trying to put what God's Word reveals together with real-life experience leads to two conclusions:

1. Emotion is an essential part of being genuinely human that adds joy and zest, and is included in our walk with God.

Life would be so cold without emotion. Billy Graham is right: "Emotion cannot be cut out of life. No intelligent person would think of saying, 'Let's do away with emotion.' Some critics are suspicious of any conversion that does not take place in a refrigerator. There are many dangers in false emotionalism, but that does not rule out true emotion and depth of feeling. Emotion may vary in religious experience. Some people are stoical and others are demonstrative, but the feeling will be there. There is going to be a tug at the heart."[3]

Who would argue against a heartfelt religion? Emotion

can no more be removed from a living faith than a person could have his or her heart cut out and live. Emotion is an essential part of being genuinely human.

2. While emotion is an essential part of life, it can be disastrous to let our feelings alone control us.

The neighborhood bully used to rule the block. What he demanded, he got. Everyone was quick to agree with the bully. No one dared to cross him, so he always got his way. Our emotions can sometimes act like that—bullying us until we forget that we can have control over them.

Our emotions do not have to be our dictator. Yet, often we make decisions based, not on careful thought, but on what we feel. We can give our emotions too much right to rule our choices, decisions, and ultimately our direction in life.

James Dobson observes, "Emotional experience in the western world has become the primary motivation of values and actions and even spiritual beliefs."[4]

Three Dangers of an Emotion-driven Life

Danger No. 1: Emotions fluctuate and therefore are not always reliable indicators of reality.

From his youth, Ron wanted to serve God. He accepted Christ at an early age and lived just to serve his Lord and Savior. He was sanctified as a teen and wanted more than anything to honor God.

Nevertheless, entering his young adult years, his life began to unravel. His emotions began to betray him, leaving him feeling hopelessly guilty. He became so depressed at times he was totally unable to function. His inability to handle his responsibilities made him feel even more guilty. Little issues would haunt Ron mercilessly. His conscience seemed supersensitive. He sought help at the altar time and again. His friends tried to encourage him. His pastor counseled him. Yet, no matter how much he prayed, no matter how many times he asked God's forgiveness, Ron was haunted by his feelings. He felt hopelessly condemned by God.

It is important to recognize that sometimes a person's

emotions can roar out of control. And it may not be a matter of lack of willpower or self-control. It may not indicate a diseased spirituality. Medical science is learning more about how the mind works and how the chemistry of the brain influences thoughts and feelings. There is increasing awareness that imbalances in the brain's chemistry can cause emotional upheavals, including serious depression, that can immobilize a person. It is tragic when spiritually sensitive persons' emotions convince them that they have lost their relationship with God because they feel so depressed.

Does depression always mean a person has lost his or her relationship with God? A seriously depressed person may certainly feel guilty. Sometimes, feeling guilty is the appropriate emotional consequence from doing wrong, but that's a different issue. When we have done wrong, the remedy for that genuine guilt is confession and repentance before God. However, some persons who have done nothing wrong may feel lost and perhaps even hopelessly separated from God. Their struggle may not be a lack of spirituality. Their problem may be a medical one. The cause of some depression is not a loss of an individual's salvation, but rather a chemical imbalance that demands medical attention from a knowledgeable physician who is able to intervene. Since emotions fluctuate and are not always reliable indicators of reality, it is dangerous to evaluate our spiritual condition based solely on how we feel.

There's a good update to Ron's story. When Ron found a knowledgeable physician who prescribed the right medication, his feelings of being forsaken by God began to disappear. Over time, he came to realize he had not lost his relationship with God, and that God had indeed never stopped loving him. When the depression lifted and emotional balance was restored, Ron regained the joy of his salvation, as well as his ability to deal with life effectively.

Danger No. 2: In an emotion-driven life, feeling-based decisions often result in bad choices.

Feeling-based decisions can keep us from doing what we

need to do. Following our feelings often leads where we don't want to go.

- ❑ The final exam is tomorrow. You need to study, but you'd rather watch TV. Your emotions say, "Watch TV." So, you see the program and flunk the final.

- ❑ Your clothes fit tighter than they should. They have not shrunk. You need to lose a few pounds, but you'd rather enjoy a big dessert. Your emotions say, "You've had a tough day. Indulge yourself." So you devour the chocolate cake, and your clothes get tighter still.

- ❑ Your wife deserves a break. The kids have been a handful. You need to take her out to a nice dinner at her favorite restaurant, but a friend calls at the last minute and invites you to complete his foursome at the golf course you've been dying to play. You know what you should do, but you also know what you want to do. (Thankfully in this case, there's no conflict. Everyone knows that thoughtful, loving husbands everywhere always would prefer to take their wives out to dinner.)

- ❑ You get a sense that your boss doesn't like you. She is often preoccupied and seldom takes time to just talk. Your emotions tell you to just avoid her. Yet, you wonder if your relationship will then grow even more distant.

In each of these examples, the common thread is the temptation to allow our choices to be determined by our emotions. It's easy to do. Still, letting our emotions drive us often means arriving at an undesirable destination. Sometimes the end is tragic. Nothing could be more dangerous than handing our lives over to the unpredictable fluctuations of our emotions.

Danger No. 3: An emotion-driven life sets believers up for spiritual collapse when tough times come.

"If we are to be defeated during life's spiritual pilgrimage, it is likely that negative emotions will play a dominant role in that discouragement," says James Dobson.[5] Negative emotions like anger, discouragement, disappointment, or bitterness are so destructive.

One person observed, "Bitterness is like drinking poison and waiting for the other person to die." Satan loves to use negative emotions like bitterness and fear to manipulate us into harmful decisions. Emotion can be a wonderful servant, but a horrible master.

Spiritual Maturity Requires Balance

In the Gospel of Matthew, Jesus said, "'Love the Lord your God with all your heart and with all your soul and with all your mind.' This is the first and greatest commandment. And the second is like it: 'Love your neighbor as yourself'" (22:37-39).

Jesus does not call us to just love with our hearts. Nor does He call us to love just with our minds. He calls us to a balanced life—heart, soul, and mind.

Jesus does not call us to turn off our emotions and stoically resign ourselves to endure whatever comes our way. Rather, He calls us to enjoy the emotions God has given us, to love God with all our hearts. What God desires is not that our emotions be forsaken nor that they tyrannize us. Rather, God desires that our emotions be submitted to Him and employed to enjoy our God-given lives. Loving God and all those around us is not a dark, empty pit to be endured, but His invitation to abundant living!

Our Model Is Jesus

In our striving to be like Jesus, we often forget to consider His emotions. Jesus reveals what it means to be fully human. His emotions reflect for us what God would have us to be.

Jesus felt compassion (Mark 1:40-41; Luke 7:13). He felt anger (Mark 3:5). He knew the pain of grief (Luke 19:41-44; John 11:35, 38). He also experienced deep joy (Luke 10:21), and never-failing love (Mark 10:21; John 11:3).

So should we.

While Jesus experienced deep emotion, His emotions were His servant, not His master.

As I write this, a wild fire rages out of control in New Mexico. Homes of horrified residents are consumed by massive flames. So far, over 47,000 acres of pristine forest have been destroyed, 405 families are homeless, and the Los Alamos nuclear weapons laboratory has been damaged. Officials hope to have the fire under control in three or four days.

Frustration grows as people reflect on the source of the fire—a "controlled burn" designed to clear away unwanted undergrowth that quickly roared out of control. It was sort of like a rock becoming dislodged on a mountain; there is no stopping the cascade once it gets out of control.

Emotions can take over like that. If we live dependent on our emotions, they can drive us where we don't want to go—making us do ugly things we never thought we'd do.

Still, there's good news! Our emotions do not have to remain the "neighborhood bully" that always gets his way. Since God offers believers the gift of self-control, we can stand up to our emotions. We can ignore their screaming, selfish demands and do what we know is right.

In offering His whole self to God (including His emotions), Jesus displayed unswerving self-control—even when He did not feel like obeying.

Imagine the emotions Jesus felt as He experienced the hours just before the Cross. He told His disciples, "My soul is overwhelmed with sorrow to the point of death" (Matthew 26:38). The hurt of betrayal. The frustration of false accusations. The anger at the blind, hard-hearted religious leaders. The anticipation of the pain and suffering. All these emotions indeed were overwhelming.

Overwhelming? Absolutely. Controlling? No. Jesus decided that instead of giving His emotions control, He would do what God commanded. "My Father," he prayed, "if it is not possible for this cup to be taken away unless I drink it, may your will be done" (v. 42). For Jesus, that meant going to the cross of Calvary. Jesus' feelings were controlled by His mind (what He knew) and His will (what He chose).

Sometimes, obedience requires that we do what we'd

rather not do. To live a God-pleasing life, our emotions must yield to our mind and our will. It requires self-control. "The fruit of the Spirit is love, joy, peace, patience, kindness, goodness, faithfulness, gentleness and self-control" (Galatians 5:22-23).

And self-control is no small matter.

Conclusion

Christians can go to one extreme and make their Christianity simply one highly emotional experience after another. Or they can go to the other extreme and make their Christianity as somber as can be. We would be right to reject either of these forms as authentic Christian faith, for Christianity is not simply a free-for-all emotional experience or a complete denial of emotion.

Mature faith is marked by intense feelings and by God-honoring choices and decisions that guide all we do. As God's people, our goal of spiritual maturity calls us to develop a balanced experience with God that offers our whole selves, including our mind, emotions, and will, to the Lordship of Jesus Christ.

Notes:

1. "Perspectives," *Newsweek*, October 11, 1999, 27.

2. James Spruce, *A Simple Faith* (Kansas City: Beacon Hill Press of Kansas City, 1986), 55.

3. "Emotions," in *Draper's Book of Quotations for the Christian World* (Fremont, Calif.: Parson Technology Software, 1992), 3052.

4. James Dobson, *Emotions: Can You Trust Them?* (Ventura, Calif.: Regal Books, 1980), 9.

5. Ibid., 11.

About the Author: Dr. Hodges is pastor of Maysville (Kentucky) Church of the Nazarene.

Common Misconception No. 12

Heard Outside the Church: "I tried Christianity once; it doesn't work."

Heard Inside the Church: "I've seen a lot of problems in the church; maybe Christianity doesn't work."

Background Scripture: Deuteronomy 6:5; Daniel 5:2, 5-6, 27; Luke 10:25, 27-28; Hebrews 12:2

CHAPTER 12

Christianity Doesn't Work

by Gene Van Note

A Muslim, one of 28,000 in a camp for refugees from Kosovo, said, "The 'Christian' Serbian soldiers came to my house in the middle of the day and forced us all outside. While one soldier held a gun on the family, the others tied up the family cow. Forcing us to watch, they carved pieces of flesh from the animal and ate as it writhed in agony. They told us to leave immediately, and we began our 51-mile trek from our home in Pristina to Skopje, with what we could carry on our backs." Then he summed up the feeling of his people: "If that's Christianity, I want nothing to do with it."[1]

Has the Muslim reached a just conclusion?

A concerned Christian talked with a man at work who claimed to have no faith in God. The Christian tried to help the man understand the benefits of knowing Jesus as Lord and, when life was over, going to heaven to be with Him for eternity.

Naming a fellow employee, the man asked, "Is he a member of your church?"

"Yes."

"If he's going to heaven, I don't want to go there."

Is that fair?

Does a person become a Christian the same way one becomes a Navajo in New Mexico, a Democrat in rural Missouri, or a "Christian" Serbian soldier? Are we born into the tribe? Is it proper to judge the tribe by what one person does in his or her weakest, angriest, or most prejudiced moments?

On the other hand, is it OK to assume we know the group on the basis of what a member does in his or her best moments?

To put it starkly, should Christianity be judged on the basis of how some of its followers act?

"No," you say.

"Why not?" the cynic answers.

That's the question we're going to explore, because many skeptics have concluded that Christianity doesn't work.

Christianity Has Been Found Wanting

On the night of October 12, 539 B.C., the Persian army diverted the Euphrates River that served as a moat around Babylon. The soldiers entered the city on the riverbed, bypassing key defensive positions. As the soldiers slipped into the city, Belshazzar was hosting a sensual feast for Babylonian society. Before the sun rose, Belshazzar was dead at the hands of the Persians, and Cyrus controlled the empire.

"What's this mean to us?" I hear you asking. "That's ancient history. It happened two and a half millennia ago."

Simply this: this history lesson illustrates an eternal truth. First, let's look at the historical record and then explore its meaning 2,500 years later.

Belshazzar's Party

King Belshazzar threw a party. And what a party it was. Before it was over, more than a thousand people were drunk on the empire's best wine. In the glow of the grape, Belshazzar ordered that the gold and silver goblets taken from the Temple in Jerusalem be brought to the feast "so that the king and his nobles, his wives and his concubines might drink from them" (Daniel 5:2).

Belshazzar did more than provide expensive goblets from which to drink. The symbolic message was, "The gods of Babylon are more powerful than the God of Israel. We are the victors; we control the world. Thus, our gods are greater than any other god in the world."

"Suddenly the fingers of a human hand appeared and

wrote on the plaster of the wall. . . . [The king's] face turned pale and he was so frightened that his knees knocked together and his legs gave way" (vv. 5-6). Minutes later, Daniel interpreted the words to the king. Daniel said, in part, "You [Belshazzar] have been weighed on the scales and found wanting" (v. 27).

Belshazzar's Imitators Across the Centuries

The judgment of Belshazzar in Daniel's day can be applied to Christianity 2,500 years later. The Muslim refugee and the fellow worker are living examples of people who have decided that Christianity is an empty religion, promising what it doesn't deliver. As far as they are concerned, Christianity has been weighed in the balances and found wanting.

To fall short implies that there is something from which to fall short. This may sound like a simple idea, but it's a pivotal thought. To be found wanting presumes there is a standard.

For example, not everyone can be an Olympic athlete. The International Olympic Committee sets qualifying standards—times and distances. An athlete can be his or her country's best and still not qualify. Run too slowly, throw the javelin not far enough, and you'll be at home watching the competition on television.

Any talk about objective ethical and moral standards is an unacceptable idea to many people in our day. We live among people who are on an inner journey to find peace, with the assumption that "whatever gods there might be" are to be found inside ourselves.

Sunday, March 12, 2000, was a pivotal day for the Roman Catholic Church. That morning at mass, Pope John Paul II said, "We humbly ask forgiveness . . . [for] the betrayal of the Gospel committed by some of our brothers over the last 2,000 years."[2] Among those actions for which the pope asked forgiveness was the failure of some Catholics to help Jews at critical times, including the violence of the Inquisition and the Crusades and, by implication, their savage treatment during the holocaust. He also asked forgiveness for Catholic lapses toward women, indigenous peoples, immigrants, the poor, and the unborn. The pope's unprecedented apology presumes a standard against which all actions can be compared.

Like Belshazzar, Christians in all ages and of every variety have been found wanting. Their conduct has fallen short of God's standard, a failing noticed by many among whom Christians lived and to whom they would take the message of salvation.

Christianity Has Been Found Difficult

Before the days of minimarts, I stopped at a mom-and-pop grocery store for a loaf of bread and a gallon of milk. The butcher said, "Are you the preacher of that little white church down the street?"

"Yes."

"I want to talk with you about one of your members, a man named Ron."[3]

As I wondered what he'd done, the butcher continued. "Ron came in here about six months ago, came around the counter, put his arm on my shoulder, and promised to pay all the money he owes. I got close enough to him to find out if he'd been drinking again, but he hadn't. He said, 'I just found Jesus as my Savior, and I want to make everything right with everybody.'

"As I listened to him talk about becoming a Christian," the butcher continued, "I said to myself, *I've heard all this before. Not from him, but from others.*

"Preacher," he said, "these people come in every once in a while and tell me they got religion and are going to pay their bills. It's sorta like a fellow who buys a new car and takes it around town to impress his friends. After a few months, the guy gets tired of paying the bill, and the dealer comes and gets his car. I figured that's what Ron would do."

Almost a century ago G. K. Chesterton, an English writer, said, "The Christian ideal has not been tried and found wanting; it has been found difficult and left untried."[4]

The Christian faith lives in tension between the conquering grace of God that forgives sin and the call to live a righteous life. We are saved by grace, and grace alone. Yet, Christianity is not like a meal at a mission, providing help with no strings attached. The free gift of God's grace brings with it certain requirements for daily living. As we've heard many preachers say, "God did not give Moses the Ten Suggestions on the holy mountain."

Christianity has its roots deep in Judaism. The Shema (pronounced shuh-MAH) is closer to the core of the faith than even the Ten Commandments. The faithful Hebrews prayed these words daily; the contemporary devout Jews have them on their lips and attached on the doorframes of their homes. "Love the LORD your God with all your heart and with all your soul and with all your strength" (Deuteronomy 6:5).

Jesus expanded this central truth when He told the story of the Good Samaritan. On that occasion, He asked the "expert in the law" (Luke 10:25) what is the meaning of life in the Law. The expert answered, "'Love the Lord your God with all your heart and with all your soul and with all your strength and with all your mind'; and, *'Love your neighbor as yourself'*" (v. 27, emphasis added). Jesus agreed with him by saying, "Do this and you will live" (v. 28).

We don't need a lot of psychobabble to know that to love our neighbors as much as we love ourselves is not the easiest item on the "To Do" list God has given us. As Chesterton said, "Christianity has been found difficult and left untried."

Christianity Has Been Found

Remember Ron?

The butcher said to me, "Several months have gone by, and Ron hasn't missed a single payment. Something happened to him. Do you know what it was?"

"I think I might," I said to the butcher. "Let me tell you about it. Or better yet, let me tell you about the One who changed Ron into the person who pays his bills."

In every generation, in all levels of society—from the poor to the rich, from the very gentle to the most aggressive—

people have been transformed by Jesus Christ. That includes a tiny woman born Agnes Gonxha Bojaxhiu, the third daughter of a construction worker in Albania, who chose to leave a comfortable life for the tired, rejected, and dying people on the streets of Calcutta. We know her as Mother Teresa. This group also includes a shoe salesman named Dwight Moody; a baseball player named Billy Sunday; a farmer's son the world knows as Billy Graham; and the illegitimate child of a geisha, Toyohiko Kagawa, Japanese evangelist and social reformer. Add to that number millions of men and women, girls and boys, who are unknown outside their communities.

None of these people has suggested that he or she is the Savior. Each has lived by the principle the writer to the Hebrews proclaimed when he said, "Let us fix our eyes on Jesus, the author and perfecter of our faith, who for the joy set before him endured the cross, scorning its shame, and sat down at the right hand of the throne of God" (12:2).

Jesus is the One who caught their attention and captured their lives. To Him they gave their allegiance and to a weary world their example. They have asked nothing but to follow their Lord and in the following share His transforming joy with their neighbors, fellow workers, family, and friends. And, if called on, to sacrifice their lives in a cause that is worth more than they can give, even if it costs that "last full measure of devotion."[5]

As they walked with Jesus on the sometimes smooth, but often broken, parts of this world, they have found a grand fellowship. These people have discovered a new community. Found a new family, a place to belong, a caring group.

The church is full of people like the song leader who, one Christmas morning, announced the next hymn. "Let's all stand and sing 'Herk, the Harold Angels Sing.'"

We smile. Mostly because *we* didn't say it. It also causes us to reflect that Christianity is made up of less-than-perfect people. Persons like the song leader, a former alcoholic, single father of two girls, fighting to keep his finances in order and his home under control.

That's one of the problems with the Church—with Christianity. Its most visible proponents are human. It doesn't take much skill to find a faulty Christian. Just hang around them for a little while. And while you're at it, see if you can't sense a new vitality, a new zest for life, a new caring for people. Perhaps you, too, will be like the lady who testified, "I've been won to the Lord by a sweet conspiracy."

Notes:
1. Teanna Sunberg, "If You Love Me . . . ," *Holiness Today*, December 1999, 10.

2. *Kansas City Star*, March 13, 2000, 1.

3. Not his real name.

4. Emily Morison Beck, ed., *Bartlett's Familiar Quotations* (Boston: Little, Brown and Company, 1980), 742.

5. Abraham Lincoln, *Gettysburg Address*, November 19, 1863.

About the Author: Rev. Van Note is a former executive editor of Sunday School curriculum for the Church of the Nazarene. He is now retired and lives in Overland Park, Kansas.

Common Misconception No. 13

Heard Outside the Church: "The Resurrection is simply a myth."

Heard Inside the Church: "The Resurrection doesn't seem very important most of the time."

Background Scripture: Genesis 1:31; 1 Kings 17:17-23; 2 Kings 4:18-37; Mark 5:21-43; Luke 7:11-15; John 11; 1 Corinthians 15; Philippians 3:7-11; 1 Thessalonians 4:13-14

483 May the Mind of Christ, My Savior

Your attitude should be the same as that of Christ Jesus. Philippians 2:5

1. May the mind of Christ, my Sav-ior, Live in me from day to day.
2. May the Word of God dwell rich-ly In my heart from hour to hour.
3. May the peace of God my Fa-ther Rule my life in ev-'ry-thing.
4. May the love of Je-sus fill me As the wa-ters fill the sea:
5. May I run the race be-fore me, Strong and brave to face the foe.
6. May His beau-ty rest up-on me As I seek the lost to win:

By His love and pow'r con-trol-ling All I do and say.
So that all may see I tri-umph On-ly thro' His pow'r.
That I may be calm to com-fort Sick and sor-row-ing.
Him ex-alt-ing, self a-bas-ing— This is vic-to-ry.
Look-ing on-ly un-to Je-sus As I on-ward go.
And may they for-get the chan-nel, See-ing on-ly Him.

WORDS: Kate B. Wilkinson, 1925
MUSIC: A. Cyril Barham-Gould, 1925

ST. LEONARDS
8.7.8.5.

CHAPTER 13

Did the Resurrection Really Happen?

by Roger Hahn

It may happen in a sociology or philosophy class at a secular school. In a seemingly offhand remark, the professor says, "And, of course, the Christian idea of the resurrection of Jesus is another example of a dying-and-rising-god myth that was common in ancient religions." The believing student in the class knows only that she had believed in the resurrection of Christ and knows nothing of ancient dying-and-rising-god myths. Assuming that the professor is knowledgeable of these matters, the believer wonders about her faith.

It may happen watching a television special or reading a newsmagazine article on the Jesus Seminar. A scholar declares, "The Resurrection stories, as part of the Gospels, are statements of faith, not history. The four Gospel accounts of the Resurrection contradict each other. They are obviously the invention of the Early Church, affirming its faith that the influence of Jesus' life continued on in their lives." The believer listening or reading knows he had always taken the Resurrection accounts literally, but a person who has obviously studied this question at great length does not. And the believer begins to question.

These two examples are a composite of the stories of many people this author has spoken with in over 25 years of ministry. Most often such believers do not quit attending church, though some do. They may continue to be active and appear to be exemplary church members, but the energy of their church life comes from social rather than theological sources. Relationships with people rather than the truth of the gospel keeps them in church. Some see the Christian faith simply as a moral system with high ethical standards. Many profess a personal relationship with Christ, but that relationship is with Jesus the ethical teacher and/or Jesus whose death on the Cross atoned for their sins. The vibrant Resurrection faith that energized the Early Church is lost in the haze of uncertainty of what a thinking Christian can and ought to believe.

The Church often contributes unwittingly to this watered-down experience of the faith. Attention to the Resurrection is reserved for Easter. Even then, the significant teaching opportunities are often muted. Frequently, Sunday School classes are dismissed and sermons canceled in favor of musical and/or dramatic presentations that rely on technical effects or musical and literary artistry to portray the Resurrection. The theological centrality and powerfully significant implications of the Resurrection are barely mentioned. Some Evangelical churches give more attention to the death of Christ on Easter Sunday than to His resurrection. It is no wonder many believers hold their faith in the Resurrection more out of duty than out of understanding and delight. We have forgotten the old saying that "every Sunday is a little Easter."

Resurrection Faith

To understand the New Testament doctrine of the Resurrection, we must distinguish the resurrection of Christ from other biblical events often called "resurrections." The so-called resurrection of Lazarus (John 11), the raising of Jairus's daughter (Mark 5:21-43), the raising of the son of the widow of Nain (Luke 7:11-15), and the similar stories of Elijah (1 Kings 17:17-23) and Elisha (2 Kings 4:18-37) bringing sons back to life all share a common story line. They bring back to normal life a person who had died. However, in every case the expectation was that the person who received life back would eventually die. These are stories of *resuscitation*.

The resurrection of Jesus was the restoration to life of a

dead man with a most significant and powerful difference. *Jesus was raised to never die again.* He was raised in or with a body but a body that is immortal. In that sense, the resurrection of Jesus is a one-of-a-kind historical event. It had never happened before; it has never happened since. The Christian faith is that it did happen once, and that someday it will happen for all believers who have died. There is very little commonality between this Christian faith and the ancient notion of dying-and-rising gods. Many ancient religions grew up in agricultural societies and focused on fertility rites. Many of them saw their gods dying and rising each year with, first, the coming of winter and, then, of spring.

The Christian hope taught in the New Testament is not that we have a never-dying soul that is released to be with God at the moment of death. That idea entered Christian thought when the gospel encountered and accommodated itself to similar Greek philosophical ideas. The New Testament is confident that believers who die will be raised to life in *bodily* form. The body will be recognizable as the same body in which we lived, but transformed into a heavenly or immortal form.

Resurrection in 1 Corinthians 15

The uniqueness of Jesus' resurrection has always made it difficult to understand—and to believe. Paul faced several objections to the Resurrection in the church at Corinth. First Corinthians 15 contains his response. The first part of the chapter (vv. 1-34) reminded them that the Resurrection is the essential truth of the gospel. The final portion of the chapter (vv. 35-58) answered Corinthian objections to the idea of a resurrected body.

Paul began by declaring that the Resurrection was the culmination of the gospel he had first preached to them. Verse 3 reminded his readers that the apostle had delivered as reliable oral teaching the exact same gospel that he had received as reliable oral teaching. Scholars believe that Paul referred to the instruction he had received right after his conversion, within just a couple of years or even a few months after the events themselves.

He presented this basic Christian message in four parts. First, Christ died for our sins, according to the Scripture. Second, He was buried. Third, He was raised the third day, according to the Scripture. Fourth, Paul listed a series of witnesses to whom Jesus appeared following His resurrection, culminating with a brief reference to his own experience with an appearance of the risen Christ. His point was that the Resurrection was an essential element of the earliest Christian preaching. It was widely attested by many witnesses who saw the risen Lord, and it was an essential element of the gospel by which the Corinthians had come to Christian faith.

We might summarize this section as saying that if Christ was not raised, then we would never have been converted.

In verses 12-19 Paul said that if the Resurrection did not happen, then Christian preaching is false and Christian faith is worthless. The problem is not simply that without the Resurrection Christian preachers would be lying to their audiences; they would also be lying about God. People in Paul's time believed that every god or goddess was concerned to protect his or her reputation. To make false claims about God would invite His severe punishment. No one would risk that for a notion as unpopular as resurrection was in the Greco-Roman world, unless the Resurrection were true. Paul maintained that the Resurrection raised Jesus to bodily existence, and unless that truth is at the center of Christian faith, there can be no meaning to the gospel. He could not imagine a form of Christianity in which faith in the Resurrection was marginal or optional.

In verses 20-28 Paul declared that Christ's resurrection was simply the first step of a process that would include a similar resurrection of believers and the final consummation of human history, when God would reign supreme over all enemies, including the ultimate enemy—death. Denying Christ's resurrection denied the future hope proclaimed by the gospel for every believer and for the whole universe. Verses 29-34 then point out that unless this resurrection hope is true, all suffering, hope, and faithfulness by believers is meaningless.

Answering Ancient Objections

The Corinthian people were influenced by Greek philosophy to believe that the body was evil and spirit (or soul) was good. Thus, for Greek philosophers, the best thing that could happen to a person was for death to destroy the evil body and for the immortal soul to survive and return to God. One sees this view powerfully effective in Socrates as he approached death. The idea that God would raise the corpses of dead people to life in bodily form was repulsive to sophisticated thinkers at Corinth. The second half of 1 Corinthians 15 answered the objection that a resurrected body is no better than our present bodies.

In verses 35-49 Paul used several illustrations to contend that the resurrection is, in fact, a bodily resurrection; but it is not the same body as we now have. By comparing the different kinds of flesh that people, animals, birds, and fish have, he proved that a body can exist without being the same as our present physical bodies. Assuming the ancient understanding of astronomy, Paul pointed to the differences between sun, moon, and stars. The differences in the light they produce represent different levels of glory. Thus resurrected bodies can still be bodies but be transformed by the resurrection. They are still recognizably bodies, but they are not subject to the same laws of physics as are our present bodies. Paul used the terms "physical body" ("natural body" in NIV) to describe our present bodies and "spiritual body" to describe the resurrection body (v. 44). The apostle did not compare the spiritual body to Christ's resurrection body, but most scholars today believe that he had in mind something similar to Christ's resurrected body when he spoke of the spiritual body that believers will receive. Christ's resurrection body was like His preresurrection body in that people could recognize Him, He could eat and drink, and there were scars from the Crucifixion. It was different in that He appeared to be able to pass through doors and walls and to move invisibly from one place to another. It was also different in that death did not lie in its future.

In verses 50-57 Paul maintained that both those who are

alive and those who have died will experience a transformation of their bodies at the resurrection. Since the resurrection body no longer dies, there is a sense in which it is superior to the physical body. At the time of the resurrection, those who have died will be raised with resurrection bodies. However, those who are still alive at the Second Coming will not be left with "deficient" physical bodies. "We will all be changed" (v. 51), declared the apostle, as he assumed that he would still be alive for that glorious transformation. He concluded the section by noting that when all this has taken place, the old enemies of sin and death will have been finally conquered. The result is that believers' labor in the Lord will not have been in vain (v. 58).

What We Can Conclude

Reflection upon Paul's teaching about the resurrection leads us to several important conclusions. First, *by means of the resurrection, God confirms His creation commitment to the human body.* Salvation *from* our bodies rather than *in* or *with* our bodies would confirm the Greek philosophical notion that bodies are evil. This would contradict God's declaration that the creation of human bodies was "very good" (Genesis 1:31).

Second, *resurrection faith demands that we take death seriously but not as an end.* Our culture is a death-denying culture. It would rather ignore death issues instead of facing the hopeless finality it brings to the non-Christian. And the church participates in it when we allow our sorrow to overwhelm the promised hope of resurrection when we lose loved ones in the Lord. We must remember what Paul told the Christians at Thessalonica: "We [are] not . . . to be ignorant about those who fall asleep, or to grieve like the rest of men, who have no hope. We believe that Jesus died and rose again and so we believe that God will bring with Jesus those who have fallen asleep in him" (1 Thessalonians 4:13-14).

A third conclusion from 1 Corinthians 15 is that *life in the body has moral significance.* How we live and how we treat our and others' bodies does matter if we are to inhabit those same bodies transformed in the future. The question naturally arises, "What about bodies disfigured by disease, or destroyed by decomposition or cremation?" The transformation process, whatever it is, will restore recognizability and normalcy to the body. By normalcy, we mean within the range of normal features—probably no "nose jobs," but perhaps restoration of lost limbs, and so on. We assume also that children born with major disfigurements will be transformed into what they would have been had the genetic and birth processes developed normally.

Victory over Sin

A related result of the truth of the Resurrection is that Christ's victory over death is also a victory over sin. Generally, the Christian faith has failed to capitalize on the significance of the Resurrection for the life and doctrine of holiness. Just as Christ's resurrection provides the possibility for our resurrection and thus our victory over death, so His resurrection provides the possibility and the power for victory over sin.

This means that Christians may—and should—live their daily lives on the basis of Resurrection hope. Paul frequently described the Christian life as union with Christ in both His death and resurrection. In Philippians 3:7-11 the apostle explained that all the sacrifices and suffering that came from following Christ were worthwhile because they enabled him to know Christ and to know the power of Christ's resurrection. The energy that enabled him to survive and persevere in the face of suffering was not merely psychological. The same power of God that raised Jesus from the dead empowered Paul to overcome suffering and to live a sacrificial, Christlike life. That experience of Resurrection power gave the apostle confidence that God would use whatever came in his future to transform him more and more into the image of Christ.

The same can happen for us today.

About the Author: Dr. Hahn is professor of New Testament at Nazarene Theological Seminary, Kansas City.